Introducti

B **etws-y-Coed**, set in a beautiful wooded the Llugwy and Conwy rivers, is the popula National Park It lies amidst a beautiful landsc; hills and mountains containing numerous h. _____os. After Thomas Telford's Waterloo Bridge over the Conwy opened in 1815, the hitherto small community became an important staging post on the London to Holyhead Irish Mail coach road. During the 19thC the stunning scenery attracted many eminent travellers, visitors and artists to this part of North Wales by road, by river as far as Trefriw, then an important inland port, and later by railway, which reached Betws-y-Coed in 1868.

The area around Betws-y-Coed and the western upland edges of the Conwy valley, lying within Snowdonia National Park, is delightful walking country, where you can quickly leave the crowds behind. The 25 circular walks in this book explore its diverse landscape and history. There are walks by rivers, past waterfalls, including the famous Swallow Falls, over hills and up Tal y Fan mountain. They follow miners' paths and waymarked trails through Gwydyr Forest Park past upland lakes and the relics of a once thriving lead-mining industry. They take you along Roman roads, past ancient upland burial chambers, standing stones and remote churches, and to great viewpoints.

The routes range from a ¾ mile visit to the famous Fairy Glen to a challenging 10 mile walk to remote lakes set beneath the Carneddau mountain range. They follow public rights of way, permissive paths, forest trails, or cross Open Access land, and are within the capability of most people. A key feature is that most individual routes, as well as containing shorter walk options, can easily be linked with others, to provide longer day walks, if required. Walking boots are recommended, along with appropriate clothing to protect against the elements. Be properly prepared and equipped, especially on the higher routes, where the weather can quickly change. Please remember that path conditions can vary according to season and weather. Contact the local Highways Department regarding any Rights of Way problems encountered. Many of the walks are accessible by regular local bus services or the Conwy Valley Railway.

Each walk has a detailed map and description which enables the route to be followed without difficulty. Bear in mind though that changes in detail can occur at any time. The location of each walk is shown on the back cover and a summary of their key features is also given. This includes an estimated walking time, but allow more time to enjoy the scenery and sights.

Please observe The Country Code and respect any ancient site visited. Enjoy your walking!

MINERS BRIDGE

DESCRIPTION A popular 1¾ mile riverside walk following the Afon Llugwy to the Miners Bridge, a favourite subject for generations of artists, returning by a quiet attractive country road. Allow about 1½ hours.

START Pont-y-Pair, Betws-y-Coed [SH 792567]

DIRECTIONS This ancient stone bridge lies just off the A5 in the centre of Betws-y-Coed, crossed by the B5106 (Trefriw).

*P**ont-y-Pair (Bridge of the Cauldron) is said to have been built across the Afon Llugwy during the 15thC by a mason called Howel, who died before its completion. Further upstream is the unusual inclined Miners Bridge, described in an 1890 book as 'a sort of ladder with rails spanning a roaring torrent', which enabled miners from Pentre Du and Rhiwddolion to get to Gwydyr's lead-mines, which were a major source of employment during the 19thC. It stands near the crossing place of the Sarn Helen Roman road.*

At the far side of the bridge turn LEFT on a minor road past Cunningham outdoor shop and a car park. Just beyond toilets, take a signposted path on the left. Go along the Tan Dinas path, soon boardwalked and raised, through Coed y Mynydd to a picnic area. Continue by the river to a ladder-stile, then along the edge of a large field to a ladder-stile. A short section of rougher wooded riverside path brings you to the Miners Bridge. Here, follow a waymarked path up through the conifers to a road. Follow this quiet country road back to Pont-y-Pair.

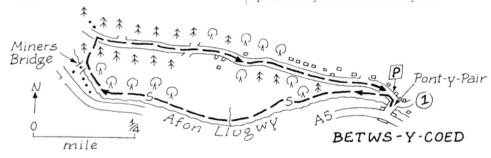

WALK 2
LLYN ELSI & SARN HELEN

DESCRIPTION A 4½ mile walk up to the attractive upland lake of Llyn Elsi, lying hidden from sight on a forested spur above the town, offering extensive views. It features a section of the Sarn Helen Roman Road, which ran from Caerhun in the Conwy Valley to Carmarthen,

the Miners Bridge and a riverside return. Allow about 2½ hours. A 4 mile walk (**B**) missing out Llyn Elsi is included.

START Pont-y-Pair, Betws-y-Coed [SH 792567] See Walk 1.

From the main road (A5) west out of Betws-y-Coed. After nearly ½ mile, go along the lane to Hendre Farm campsite. Cross a stile by a gate at the camping field entrance and go up the wide enclosed path

to a ladder-stile into a wood. The path rises steadily through the trees to reach the bend of a forestry track. Cross a nearby stile by a gate and go up a stony path, soon passing an old tramway on your right. Continue up the path, soon bending left past the former 19thC Hafod-las slate quarry to a ladder-stile. Go up the path, soon emerging onto the open hillside to cross a

Miners Bridge A5

0   ¼ mile

Sarn Helen

N

walk 3

quarry

③

④

alk

monument

Llyn Elsi

① BETWS-Y-COED

gate. Follow the waymarked path up and across a small grassy ridge – *offering good mountain views* – then past a small reedy area, before gradually bending LEFT down to the nearby forest perimeter. The wide path descends then heads away from the forest to gates to join a stony track beyond. (The next section to the A5 follows the former Sarn Helen Roman road.)

4 Follow the track down to a house, then its access lane down to a stony forestry track. Go through the gate opposite and one just below, then follow the delightful enclosed stony path down to a cross-track below a house. Continue ahead down the stony path, cross a footbridge then a stile and follow the track down to join a road leading to the A5. Follow the signposted path opposite to cross the Miners Bridge, then follow the riverside path back to Pont-y-Pair.

stile by a barn above. Follow a signed path up an old track to eventually reach a wide path angling in on the left. (For **Walk B** keep ahead along the track to an access track by Hafod Las. Follow it left to a ladder-stile/gate and up to a wide forestry track. Follow it right to point **3**.)

2 For Llyn Elsi, turn LEFT and follow the signed path to a ladder-stile, and on near a wall then up through an area of small trees to a forestry track. Continue with a path opposite through more small trees to reach a waymarker post at a stony cross path. Follow it LEFT up to the monument above Llyn Elsi. *It was erected to commemorate the opening of the Betws-y-Coed waterworks in 1914, when the lake became a reservoir providing water for the town. Good views of Moel Siabod and the Carneddau mountains.* Return down the path and past your outward path. Just before a footbridge near the dam turn RIGHT along a stony path through trees to reach the stony forestry track crossed earlier. Follow it LEFT.

3 After ⅓ mile cross a ladder-stile on the left by the gated entrance to Pant yr hyddod. Go along its stony access track and as you near the house go up a waymarked path to pass behind the barn to a kissing

Miners Bridge

WALK 3

LLYN ELSI

DESCRIPTION A 6 mile walk (**A**) exploring the attractive part-wooded upland area above Betws-y-Coed containing the beautiful hidden lake of Llyn Elsi. The route follows a waymarked white forestry trail up to Llyn Elsi, then follows the trail in reverse around the lake. After enjoying extensive views from the commemorative monument, the route meanders down through old quarry workings and woodland to cross the Miners Bridge for a delightful riverside return. Allow about 3½ hours. The route can be shortened to a 4¾ mile walk (**B**) by going direct to the monument.

START Car park by toilets, near the railway station, Betws-y-Coed [SH 795565] – both signposted from the main A5 road.

From the southern end of the car park follow a pathway past the toilets to cross the main road. Turn RIGHT past the PO/ stores, then LEFT up a road, soon bearing RIGHT beneath Church Hill House and above St Mary's church. At a Gwydr Forest Park information board, marking the start of two forestry trails, head up to a barrier gate into the wood. Now follow the waymarked white/ blue trails up a stony forestry track. Later when the track splits, continue up the RIGHT fork on the waymarked white trail. Follow the trail through several track junctions up to a bend overlooking Llyn Elsi, with a good view of Moel Siabod. (For **Walk B** turn right and follow the waymarked stony trail path up to the monument above the lake.)

2 The main walk now follows the track LEFT along the eastern side of the lake. Just beyond the end of the lake the track descends. When it bends left, go past a waymarker post on the right up a stony path. Follow the undulating trail path, soon heading north through an area of birch. After crossing a turning area continue along a forestry track – *with a brief view of Llyn Elsi*. Shortly the track bends west towards Moel Siabod, where it overlooks a narrow arm of the lake. Here, at a waymarker post on the right go down the stony trail path to cross

a footbridge and continue near the water's edge to reach a prominent viewpoint across the lake – *a good place to stop to watch the wildfowl and dragonflies*. The path now meanders round the western side of the lake to the dam. Here go up steps and descend to a footbridge over the lake's outlet to reach a path junction below the dam. Keep ahead and follow the stony path up to a monument and seats. *It was erected to commemorate the opening of the Betws-y-Coed waterworks in 1914, when the lake became a reservoir providing water for the town. There are good views from Moel Siabod to the Carneddau mountains.* Return down the path.

3 At the bottom of the slope, turn RIGHT along a waymarked path through an area of small trees to a forestry track. Go down a path opposite through another area of small trees, then alongside a wall, to a ladder-stile. Follow the signed path to an old track with a stone barn visible ahead. Here turn sharp RIGHT and follow another signed path down the track to cross a stile by a barn. Turn LEFT down the path, through an old gateway and down through trees to a ladder-stile. Continue down the path past the former 19thC Hafod-las slate quarry, soon bending right. After 50 yards, at a gate at the end of the wall on the right turn LEFT along a former tramway.

4 At a facing gate, descend a path to cross a stream leading from a mine adit, and continue between spoil heaps and past two small quarry buildings. Just beyond the second building, descend the path to cross a stile on the left. Go up the field edge by nearby spoil heaps to a stile into a wood. Follow the path through the trees to reach a track. Follow it LEFT. At a track junction below a house keep ahead on the track to cross a stream. About 100 yards further, at a large rock slab turn RIGHT down a path towards the nearby small waterfall, then continue down through the wood, initially near the stream to a small parking area. Turn RIGHT down the minor road past houses to the A5. Follow the signposted path opposite, soon descending steps to cross the Miners Bridge – *just as miners would have done on their way to work in the lead-mines during the 19thC.*

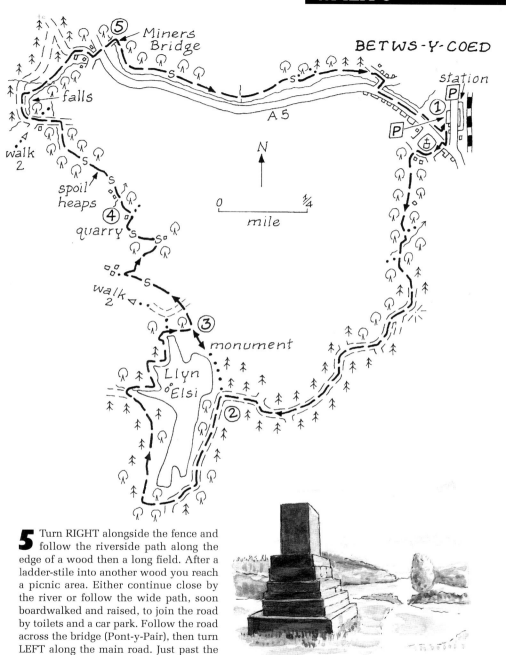

BETWS-Y-COED

Miners Bridge

station

falls

walk 2

A5

N

0 — ¼
mile

spoil heaps

quarry

④

walk 2

③

monument

Llyn Elsi

②

5 Turn RIGHT alongside the fence and follow the riverside path along the edge of a wood then a long field. After a ladder-stile into another wood you reach a picnic area. Either continue close by the river or follow the wide path, soon boardwalked and raised, to join the road by toilets and a car park. Follow the road across the bridge (Pont-y-Pair), then turn LEFT along the main road. Just past the Royal Oak Hotel, take a path through the park back to the start.

Llyn Elsi monument

WALK 4

LLUGWY & LLEDR VALLEYS

DESCRIPTION An 8 mile walk linking the beautiful wooded Llugwy and Lledr valleys. The route follows the riverside path to the Miners Bridge, then takes Sarn Helen, the former Roman road to Mid-Wales, up across the part-wooded hillside, reaching a height of about 800 feet/250 metres, before descending into the Lledr valley. Further delightful riverside walking is followed by a climb up the initially steep wooded slopes to Llyn Elsi for a final descent through the forest. Allow about 5 hours. The route can be undertaken as two linear walks from Pont-y-Pant halt – a request stop on the Betws-y-Coed – Blaenau Ffestiniog railway line: a 4 mile return via Sarn Helen, or a 4½ mile return via Llyn Elsi following the route from point **3**.

START Car park/toilets near the Railway Station, Betws-y-Coed [SH 795565] – both signposted from the main A5 road.

From the toilets follow the pathway round the edge of the recreational area to join the main road by the Royal Oak Hotel. Shortly, turn RIGHT on the B5106 (Trefriw) across the bridge (Pont-y-Pair) over the river, then LEFT. Just beyond a car park/toilets go along the Tan Dinas path to a picnic area. Now follow the riverside path to a ladder-stile, and along the edge of a large field, then woodland to the Miners Bridge. Descend the inclined bridge, go up steps and follow the path ahead to the A5. Go along the road opposite. At its end by Bryn Tirion follow an old narrow enclosed track (Sarn Helen) ahead to a gate. Continue up the track then path to a stile/gate, over a footbridge and up to a track junction. Keep ahead past the nearby house, then follow the delightful enclosed stony path up to a forestry track. Go up the narrow lane opposite to a house. Continue up the narrow rough lane, soon becoming a stony track.

2 Just beyond a small ruin, the track descends and continues to a gate. *Nearby are the ruined houses of Rhiwddolion – a once thriving community that was abandoned during the early 20thC following the closure of local mines and quarries.* Continue up the track and on past the forest to a gate. The track goes through conifers then an area of birch trees, crosses a forestry track, and continues to a ladder-stile/gate. Follow the track across open country – *with good views across the wooded Lledr valley* – later descending to join a lane. Follow it down into the Lledr valley. After a house (Ty Llwyd), cross a stile and follow the waymarked path across its garden to the A470. Take the road opposite over the Afon Lledr beneath Plas Hall Hotel.

3 At the junction, follow the road LEFT behind the hotel and down to the entrance to the Lledr Hall Outdoor Education Centre. Keep ahead down the enclosed path, across the driveway, and through a gate ahead. The path now passes beneath the hidden railway line, briefly joins the river, then soon runs near a wall. It continues close to the river and railway and passes through a small metal gate, then a wooden gate at a waymarked path junction. Here, turn LEFT and follow the waymarked path through woodland, then past a river gorge, and on to a ladder-stile. Follow the riverside path to Tan Aeldroch farm, then turn LEFT down its access track to a stile/gate on the right. Follow the track through the riverside campsite and continue through the next field to a stile at its end. Follow the path up through trees and on to pass under the railway arch. Go past a ladder-stile and follow the path alongside the fence, soon bending right between the fence and a wall to reach cottages.

6

4 Here turn sharp LEFT along a green track to pass behind the larger cottage. When the walled track bends right go through the old gateway ahead. Follow a path to cross a large

BETWS-Y-COED

A5

Miners Bridge

Afon Llugwy

station

Sarn Helen

walk 2

Rhiwddolion

Afon Lledr

monument

Llyn Elsi

N

0 ¼ mile

Afon Lledr

steep and crossing the stream. At a forestry track, take a level path opposite through the trees. Later it rises past a small ruin, soon being joined by a less distinct path coming in from another ruin to your left. Beyond a stream the path rises then continues past a short section of wall and through trees to emerge on a forestry track by hidden Llyn Elsi. Follow it RIGHT up and along the lake's eastern side. On the bend follow the waymarked white trail path ahead along the edge of the lake up to the monument.

5 Looking north, of three waymarked paths, take the one leading RIGHT, soon rising and continuing through the young forest, then descending to a forestry track. Follow the path opposite through the forest to another track, then descend a stony path to pass ruins. The path now zig-zags down the wooded slope, then crosses a footbridge to reach the waymarked Llyn Elsi trail track. Follow it down through the forest to reach the road behind St Mary's church. Follow it RIGHT down to the main road and back to the start.

footbridge over the river, then through the trees to the A470. Cross the road and follow it with care under nearby Pont Gethin – *the railway viaduct built in 1875 – 78 by Gethin, a local builder* – then turn RIGHT along the track leading to Craig Lledr. After about 40 yards, take a signposted path on the left. It angles up through the trees, crosses a footbridge, then rises steeply up the wooded slope near the stream, later becoming less

FAIRY GLEN

DESCRIPTION A choice of short walks, easily combined, near the famous Fairy Glen, a deep narrow wooded river gorge, popular since Victorian times. **Walk A** follows a delightful ¾ mile privately owned circular trail to the Fairy Glen, with a nominal charge payable. **Walk B** is an enjoyable there and back 1½ mile popular Victorian stroll towards Conwy Falls along the former London to Holyhead tollgate road, superseded by Telford's new road (A5) in the early 19thC, and now a track/path. Continuing to the entrance to Conwy Falls nowadays involves walking on the busy A5, with no pavement and tight bend, and is not recommended!

START Fairy Glen car park [SH 799546]

DIRECTIONS Just south of Waterloo Bridge, Betws-y-Coed, take the A470 towards Dolgellau/Dolwyddelan. Just before Beaver Bridge over the river, turn left up a track signposted 'Fairy Glen car park/Cymanog Isaf Farm' to a car park (small charge payable).

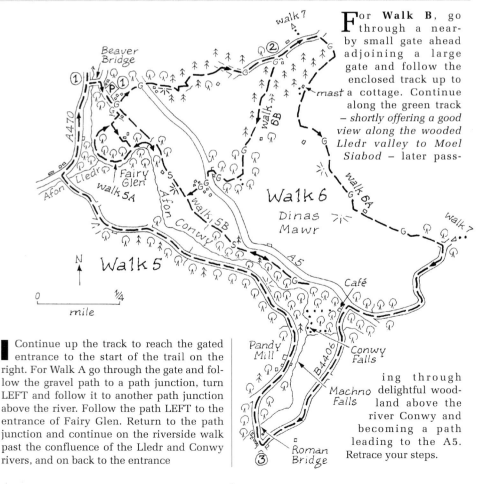

For **Walk B**, go through a nearby small gate ahead adjoining a large gate and follow the enclosed track up to a cottage. Continue along the green track – *shortly offering a good view along the wooded Lledr valley to Moel Siabod* – later pass-

Continue up the track to reach the gated entrance to the start of the trail on the right. For Walk A go through the gate and follow the gravel path to a path junction, turn LEFT and follow it to another path junction above the river. Follow the path LEFT to the entrance of Fairy Glen. Return to the path junction and continue on the riverside walk past the confluence of the Lledr and Conwy rivers, and on back to the entrance

ing through delightful woodland above the river Conwy and becoming a path leading to the A5. Retrace your steps.

WALK 6

DINAS MAWR, CONWY & MACHNO FALLS

DESCRIPTION A varied 5 mile walk (**A**) which combines well with the Fairy Glen trail. The route rises from the Conwy Valley, initially through woodland, to follow a delightful old track across attractive upland country adjoining the dominant crag of Dinas Mawr, offering extensive views. After descending to the Conwy Falls Café, with the option of visiting Conwy falls (small charge), it then follows a scenic quiet country road past an ancient packhorse bridge, Machno falls and the Conwy gorge. Allow about 3 hours. An alternative 2 mile walk (**B**) is described.

START From the minor road near Beaver Bridge [SH 798547], or as Walk 5 if you are also visiting Fairy Glen.

Cross beaver Bridge, then turn RIGHT up a track signposted to Fairy Glen/Cymanog Isaf to Fairy Glen car park. Continue up the track and go through a bridle gate opposite the Fairy Glen trail entrance. Follow the enclosed path up past the house to the A5. Cross the road with care to go through a wall gap by the entrance to Bron Haul. Follow a path up along the wood edge beside a wall. The path then zig-zags up the wooded slope and continues up to join a wall, which it follows up to an old forestry track. Follow it RIGHT then continue up a minor road to pass a small conifer wood. (For **Walk B**, at the wood corner go through a kissing gate. Follow the path alongside the wall, over a stream, soon alongside another wall, then down to a kissing gate. Descend the part tree-covered slopes leading to nearby Dinas Mawr, soon more steeply through trees past a telegraph post. Just below it, at a path junction, bear RIGHT down through bracken then trees, soon near a fence, to a kissing gate. Follow the path down to the nearby A5 – caution! Cross the road to the pavement opposite. Turn LEFT, then follow the signposted path down a gated track. At old buildings, turn RIGHT down the waymarked path to a small metal gate. Go down past the first of other old buildings, through a gateway and follow an old green track down the field to an old enclosed green cross track. Follow it RIGHT past a cottage and back to the start.

2 For **Walk A** continue along the road past a cottage, then at a gate across the road, follow a signposted path RIGHT up a green track near a wall to a gate at the wood corner. Continue up the green track and on alongside the wood's perimeter wall, soon passing a radio transmitter mast near the wood corner. Continue along the gated green track across scenic undulating rugged upland pasture – *enjoying extensive valley and mountain views* – past the nearby bracken covered rocky top of Dinas Mawr and on down to a minor road. Follow it down to the A5. Cross the road with care to reach the nearby junction. Turn LEFT on the B4406 towards Penmachno. *Nearby is the Conwy Falls Café and access to the waterfalls.* Follow the road across the Conwy gorge and on for about ½ mile.

3 At crossroads by cottages, turn RIGHT to pass the former Penmachno Woollen Mill – *built originally in the 1830s as a fulling mill powered by water from the adjoining Afon Machno. Just downstream is the 17thC-packhorse bridge, known as 'Roman Bridge'.* Follow the road to Pandy Mill, opposite which a path leads past the ruined corn mill to nearby Machno Falls. Continue along the road, past a viewpoint of the Conwy gorge and later with Dinas Mawr towering above the valley. *Dinas Mawr greatly impressed George Borrow, which he described as 'an immense mountain' in his famous book 'Wild Wales', when he walked beneath it in 1854.* Eventually, the road descends to cross the 15thC Pont-ar-Lledr to reach the A470. Cross the road and follow a walkway/cycleway RIGHT to Beaver Bridge and the nearby start.

MYNYDD GARTHMYN & CAPEL GARMON BURIAL CHAMBER

DESCRIPTION A 6½ mile walk (**A**) exploring the attractive upland area to the east of Betws-y-Coed, featuring a classic viewpoint overlooking the town and the Conwy valley from Mynydd Garthmyn (823 feet/251 metres), the old droving village of Capel Garmon, and an impressive Neolithic burial chamber. Allow about 4 hours. The route offers an alternative 4½ mile walk (**B**), and a 2¾ mile walk (**C**), missing out the burial chamber. This walk can easily be accessed from Betws-y-Coed via Walk 8.

START Lay-by on A470 near Waterloo Bridge [SH 799560].

DIRECTIONS After leaving Betws-y-Coed via Waterloo Bridge, turn left on the A470 towards Llanwrst to park in the second lay-by on the left.

1 Continue along the roadside pathway, then take the road signposted to Capel Garmon. Follow it up the wooded hillside, later passing a house and signposted path on the right. Just past a row of terraced cottages go through a kissing gate on the left. Continue ahead up steps and past Garmonfa, then turn LEFT along the access track to a ladder-stile at the entrance to Pen-y-Foel. Briefly follow its access track, then take a waymarked path on the right. Follow it through an area of birch, rowan, bracken, heather and gorse – *with good views of Moel Siabod, the Glyders, Tryfan and the Carneddau Mountains* – to a stile.

2 A few yards beyond angle LEFT to follow a wide path up the slope, then after 15 yards take a narrow path angling LEFT, soon continuing north below a small rocky ridge on your right to reach a small pool. Go up onto the nearby crag to a superb viewpoint overlooking Betws-y-Coed. Afterwards go past the southern end of the pool, up the slope ahead, then up a path angling LEFT. When the path levels out – *with a view of wind turbines ahead* – work your way up to a visible waymarker post onto the impressive rocky summit of Mynydd Garthmyn for superb all-round views. Descend south-west, passing a group of trees to your right, to join your outward route. Return to the road. (For **Walk C** go back down the road, then take the signposted path on the left over the stream. Go along the right fork of the track to rejoin the main route at point **6**.)

3 Turn LEFT and follow the road past the entrance to boarding kennels/cattery and a house. Just past Garthmyn, go through a kissing gate on the right. Angle LEFT across the field to another kissing gate, then continue ahead across the next field to a kissing gate onto an access track. *Capel Garmon with its church is prominent ahead.* Go through a small gate opposite and continue to a waymarker post just to the left of a clump of trees ahead to a kissing gate beyond. Cross the paved path then go up the field and past the front of nearby cottages. At the garden wall corner, turn LEFT up alongside the wall to a kissing gate in the corner. Turn RIGHT and angle away from the fence up towards the church, then follow the churchyard wall LEFT to reach the road opposite the school via a kissing gate. *The village stands on an old drovers' route along which sheep and cattle once passed on their way to market at Llanrwst or further afield in England.* Follow the road through the village past the 19thC church and the White Horse Inn to a junction by a chapel. (For **Walk B** turn right and follow the road to point **5**.)

4 Follow the road ahead out of the village – *enjoying good views west.* After passing two access tracks the road begins to rise. Take a signposted Snowdonia National Park path through a kissing gate on the right. Follow the waymarked path to Tyn-y-Coed farm. Go through the farmyard and up its access lane. On the bend turn RIGHT down to a finger post and go through a nearby small gate. Go along the field edge, and through post and follow the path LEFT alongside a boundary down to a stile. Continue down the field edge, over a ladder-stile and down through the wood to another ladder-stile onto a green track. Turn LEFT, then immediately RIGHT through a wall gap onto another track by a cottage. Follow it LEFT.

a gate in the boundary. Angle LEFT across the field to reach the burial chamber. Go through a nearby kissing gate, then about 30 yards beyond angle LEFT up to a waymarker post on the small rocky ridge. Continue up through trees and on to a finger post. Turn RIGHT down a green track to a gate. Continue down the track, then follow the signposted diverted path down the slope to a minor road. Turn RIGHT down the road, then after a gate turn RIGHT along a track. Follow the gated green track up across scenic undulating rugged upland pasture – *enjoying extensive mountain views.* Just before a radio transmitter station, take the track's waymarked right fork and follow it alongside the wood to a gate at its corner, then down to a minor road. Turn LEFT.

5 After about 100 yards, with a cottage just ahead, cross a stile on the right. Keep ahead, past a nearby stile and on up between a wall and a fence to a ladder-stile. Follow the path ahead, then at a finger post bear RIGHT, soon alongside a wall, then briefly descending past a small tree encrusted crag. At a waymarked path junction keep ahead, then at the next go up to a nearby small gate at the end of a stone barn. Follow the waymarked path through the boarding kennels/cattery and continue up its driveway. Shortly, angle LEFT on a waymarked path, soon reaching a kissing gate. Follow the waymarked path down to a stile above a gate. Descend to a waymarker

6 On the bend, take a signposted path on the right. Follow it down the wooded slope alongside a wall, over a track, and on down to suddenly emerge on the A5 alongside the Ty Gwyn Hotel (caution). Cross the road. Turn RIGHT back to the start.

11

WALK 8

ST MICHAEL'S CHURCH

DESCRIPTION A 2¾ mile figure of eight (**A**) or shorter 1½ mile (**B**) walk exploring the fine riverside scenery at Betws-y-Coed and featuring the 14thC St Michael's church, which served as the parish church until the larger St Mary's was built to accommodate the religious needs of 19thC tourists. The route follows the Afon Llugwy to its confluence with the Afon Conwy, which it then accompanies to the church. Walk A crosses the river by a delightful suspension bridge and follows a path to the road for a return across the attractive cast-iron Waterloo Bridge built in 1815 by Thomas Telford to carry the London-Holyhead road. Allow about 1½ hours.

START Railway Station, Betws-y-Coed. [SH 795565] – signposted from the main A5 road.

From the clock at the railway station entrance, take a nearby pathway signposted to the National Park Centre/ Tourist Information Centre. Go past the Centre's arched entrance then follow a signposted path through a gate and along the lane to Royal Oak Farm. Continue along a stony footpath, soon alongside the river Llugwy, to pass under the railway bridge. Follow the riverside path along the perimeter of the golf course to where it joins the Conwy river. Continue on the signposted path beside the Afon Conwy as it meanders southwards along the other edge of the golf course, later joining a lane. On its bend, cross a stone stile and go through the edge of St Michael's churchyard to its entrance. (For **Walk B**, turn right along the road to access the railway station via the tempting Buffet Coach cafe, Conwy Valley Railway Shop/ Museum, and footbridge over the railway line.)

2 For **Walk A**, cross the nearby suspension bridge over the river. *It was built in 1930, after the destruction by floods of a*

bridge constructed by the Royal Engineers in WW1 as a replacement for stepping stones just downstream. Follow the enclosed path to a farm and up its driveway to the road. Turn RIGHT and follow the roadside pathway to the junction. Turn RIGHT over Waterloo Bridge and follow the road into Betws-y-Coed, then go along Ffordd hen Eglwys, signposted to the Railway Museum/golf course. Follow the road over the railway line and on to reach St Michael's church, where you join Walk B to reach the nearby railway station.

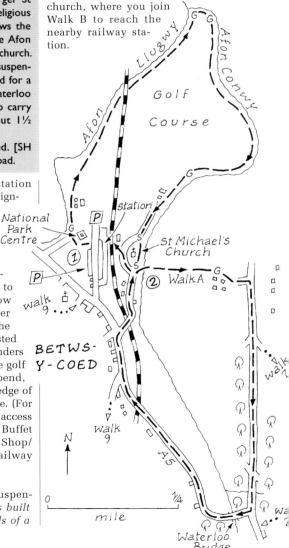

12

WALK 9

CLOGWYN GIGFRAN

DESCRIPTION A 3¾ mile walk following a waymarked forestry trail through Gwydyr Forest Park above Betws-y-Coed, reaching a height of 722 feet/220 metres with good views across the Conwy and Lledr valleys. Allow about 2 hours.

START Car park by toilets opposite the Railway Station and shops, Betws-y-Coed [SH 795565].

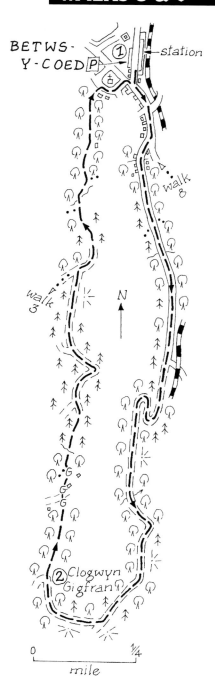

1 Go to the main road and turn LEFT. Go across the road signposted to the Railway Museum (Ffordd hen Eglwys), then take a road on the right passing behind Cotswold outdoor shop. Follow the road past Betws-y-Coed Motors then through majestic mature woodland for about ½ mile. Just before the railway bridge, follow the waymarked blue trail up a stony forestry track on the right. It rises steadily up the wooded hillside eventually passing a viewpoint over the upper Conwy valley, after which it bends into the Lledr valley. Later the track reaches another viewpoint by a green track at Clogwyn Gigfran (Giant's Head) overlooking the river and railway line below, after which it climbs away from the valley.

2 When the track bends sharp left, turn RIGHT and follow the waymarked blue trail/path through an area of open woodland to a footbridge and small gate. Keep ahead to an access track leading to a nearby house. Go through a gate opposite and follow the waymarked blue trail/path, briefly alongside the fence, then up to a small gate to join an old forestry track above. Follow it RIGHT up to a junction, then bear RIGHT down the track. When it splits follow the blue trail down the right fork – *soon with a view across the wooded Conwy valley.* Shortly you are joined by the white forestry trail from Llyn Elsi. Continue down the track, eventually leaving the forest to reach the road behind St Mary's church. Follow it RIGHT down to the main road and back to the start.

13

LLYN PARC

DESCRIPTION A 7 mile figure of eight walk (**A**) utilising three waymarked forest trails to explore the attractive mature mixed woodland of Gwydyr Forest Park, featuring the hidden upland lake of Llyn Parc and prominent view-points. The route initially crosses the wooded hillside beneath Clogwyn Cyrau escarpment then climbs Aberllyn Ravine past old mine workings and continues past Llyn Parc. After descending in stages to a forestry car park (an alternative start), the route heads south, later climbing to pass the end of Llyn Parc, then returning down another forest trail. Allow about 4 hours. The route includes three shorter walks of 4¼ miles (**B**), 2¾ miles (**C**) and 1½ miles (**D**). The alternative start offers a 4¼ mile walk to Llyn Parc.

START Pont-y-Pair, Betws-y-Coed [SH 792567] or Forestry car park [SH781609].

DIRECTIONS This ancient stone bridge lies just off the A5 in the centre of Betws-y-Coed. The alternative start is accessed from the B5106.

I At the far side of the bridge turn LEFT along a minor road past a car park and toilets. Shortly, take a road on the right, which soon bends left up past wooden houses and becomes a stony track as it enters the forest. Take the signposted blue and white forestry trail on the right, and at the path junction, turn RIGHT signposted 'Cyrau'. Follow the waymarked white trail up through the trees, soon passing beneath craggy Clogwyn Cyrau and descending to a viewpoint overlooking Betws-y-Coed. Keep away from the cliff edge. The undulating path continues through mixed woodland, later descending to a crossroad of paths. (For **Walk D** turn right and follow the yellow/white waymarked path, then track down to the road.)

2 Turn LEFT to join the waymarked Llyn Parc yellow trail which you will follow for the next few miles. The path rises, later more steeply up the edge of the narrowing

Aberllyn Ravine above the stream to reach the top of a small waterfall. *The sealed mine entrances, debris and ruins are relics of lead and zinc mines that were worked here during the 18thC until their abandonment early last century.* After crossing a footbridge over the stream, continue along the forest edge, past a nearby cottage and follow a narrow track to reach a stony forestry track with a seat ahead at the end of Llyn Parc. (For **Walk C** turn left to point **5**.) *The water level of this sheltered remote lake is now much lower than when it provided water power for the mines. Today, despite its life-restricting high-level mineral content, it is a peaceful place to watch the dragonflies skimming its surface.*

3 Bear RIGHT along the track. Shortly, follow the waymarked yellow trail LEFT down through trees then along the wooded edge of the lake, later bending up to rejoin the stony forestry track. (For **Walk B** turn right and follow the track back past the southern end of the lake to point **5**.) Follow it LEFT, then at a junction take the track's LEFT fork (yellow trail), descending steadily past Marin bike trails. At a crossroad of tracks, turn RIGHT up the yellow trail. After 50 yards, the trail angles off the track, continues through trees and crosses a bike trail. Shortly afterwards the yellow trail bends right and continues below a green track. At a way-marked path junction the yellow trail turns sharp LEFT and descends to the top tier of a car park. Turn RIGHT past a Marin Mountain Bike Trail Information Board.

4 Go past the barrier ahead and along the stony track on the yellow/white walks trails – *soon enjoying extensive views along the Conwy Valley and across to Llanrwst.* When the track splits keep on the upper fork to follow the yellow trail past side paths to reach a picnic area at a prominent viewpoint. At a nearby track junction keep ahead on the yellow trail. The narrow track rises steadily, later passing an open aspect with views into the Conwy valley, with the river below. The track becomes a stony path, rising steadily, then does a sharp U-turn up through trees and continues along an improving narrow track to reach a junction of tracks. Turn LEFT

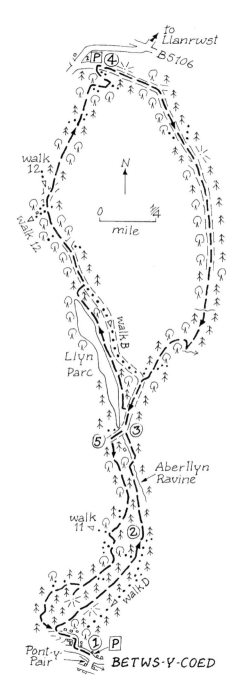

Pont-y-pair

along the wide stony forestry track, soon joining your outward route, to reach the end of the Llyn Parc at point 3. Keep ahead up the forestry track.

5 After about 60 yards, turn LEFT past a green forestry post and follow a path (blue trail) through trees. It soon descends to a small ruin, then rises before continuing across a more open aspect. The blue trail then continues along a narrow stony track shared with a Marin bike trail. After about 120 yards you reach a blue Marin post. *A few yards further is a good view of Moel Siabod.* Here the blue trail descends LEFT through trees to a green track. Follow it LEFT. Shortly, the blue trail turns RIGHT. First continue ahead, and as the path begins to descend, take a path angling LEFT to reach a crag overlooking Betws-y-Coed. Return to follow the blue trail up to pass round a fenced-off old mine, then along the edge of a replanted area of forest, soon descending through trees to a path junction. Here, the blue trail descends LEFT through conifers, later passing a seat to join your outward route back to the start.

LLYN SARNAU & LLANRWST MINE ENGINE HOUSE

DESCRIPTION A 5½ mile walk (**A**) exploring Gwydyr Forest Park on good paths and tracks, incorporating part of a waymarked forest trail. The route climbs to a high viewpoint on Clogwyn Cyrau overlooking the town, before meandering across the part-wooded upland area, with extensive mountain views, to visit the 19thC Llanrwst mine engine-house, with surviving chimney, and passing Llyn Sarnau, an upland reservoir that once provided water for local lead-mines. After descending into the Llugwy valley, the route offers a road or riverside return from the Miners Bridge. Allow about 3½ hours. A shorter 4 mile walk (**B**) is included.
START Pont-y-Pair, Betws-y-Coed [SH 792567].
DIRECTIONS This ancient stone bridge lies just off the A5 in the centre of Betws-y-Coed, crossed by the B5106 (Trefriw).

1 At the far side of the bridge turn LEFT on a minor road past a car park and toilets. Continue up the single track road, then turn RIGHT up a no through road on the way-marked forest trails. Shortly the road bends LEFT up past wooden houses and becomes a stony track as it enters the forest. Take the signposted blue and white forest trail on the right, and at the path junction keep ahead on the blue trail (Pen-yr-Allt). The trail path angles steeply across the wooded slope to a seat, then rises through conifers, the gradient gradually easing. At a path junction turn RIGHT up the blue trail, along the edge of a replanted area of forest, then down past a fenced-off old mine and on to reach a green track. Before following the blue trail left, first turn RIGHT, and as the ground begins to descend, take a path angling LEFT to reach a crag on Clogwyn Cyrau overlooking Betws-y-Coed. Return to follow the blue trail/green track through the wood. At the bend of the track follow the blue trail RIGHT up through trees to a narrow stony track by a blue Marin post.

2 Here you leave the blue trail, by turning LEFT, soon passing a ruined house – *with a good view of Moel Siabod.* Follow the track through mixed woodland. When it splits, take the right fork, then continue ahead up the stony forestry track. At the next junction, turn LEFT, now rejoining the blue trail. Shortly, follow the waymarked blue trail/path LEFT up through trees, soon descending. When the path splits you have a choice. (For **Walk B** follow the waymarked blue trail left fork to a stile at the wood edge, then follow the blue trail between two stone barns and along a green track to pass in front of Coed Mawr to cross a ladder-stile. Follow the trail across the meadow – *with a view now of Tryfan and the Carneddau mountains* – to a stile, then along an enclosed path to a ladder-stile and down to a forestry track to rejoin Walk A. Turn LEFT and resume instructions at paragraph 4.)

3 For **Walk A** take the right fork to a nearby forestry track. Follow it LEFT past the dam of a small reservoir to a track junction. Continue ahead up the track, then at the top of the rise angle RIGHT up a side track. Follow it down past a cottage – *enjoying excellent views across the Llugwy valley to Moel Siabod, the Glyders, and the Carneddau mountains.* Later as the stony track bends left towards a nearby crossroad of tracks, turn RIGHT along an old narrow track through trees to reach a stony forestry track. Cross the ladder-stile opposite and go along the signposted path. At a waymarker post turn RIGHT and follow the path to Llanrwst lead-mine engine house – *built in 1876/77 to pump water from the mine.* Return to the ladder-stile, then follow the track RIGHT down to a track junction. Turn LEFT and follow the stony track past Llyn Sarnau to a crossroad of tracks. Continue ahead along the track, soon enjoying extensive views. Shortly, go down the right fork of the track to rejoin the blue trail near an area of old workings.

4 Continue along the stony forestry track, past a side track, then cross a ladder-stile on the right in an open aspect. Follow the blue trail ahead to a stile, along the edge of a wood to another stile, then down past a stone barn – *enjoying good views of Moel Siabod, Snowdon, then the Glyders and Tryfan.* Cross an access track leading to a nearby cottage, and follow the waymarked trail ahead down to a ladder-stile into the forest. After a short steep descent requiring care, the path widens and angles steadily down through the trees to reach a minor road. Either follow the road LEFT back to the start, or take the signposted path opposite angling down to the Miners Bridge, and return along the riverside path.

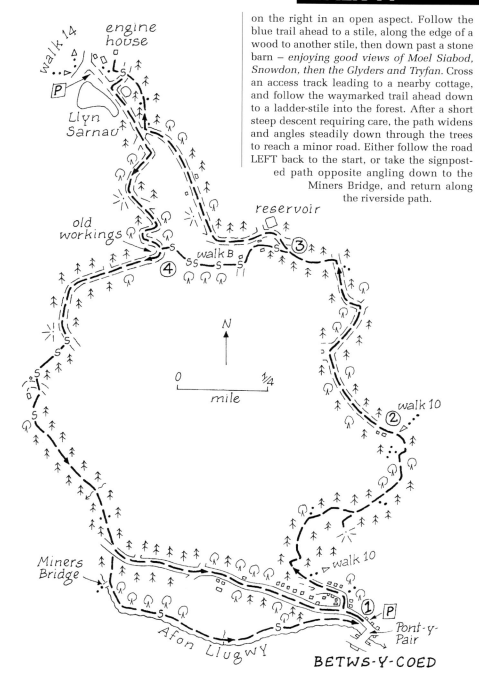

HAFNA MINE

DESCRIPTION A 3½ mile walk **(A)** exploring the remains of the once thriving lead-mining industry that dominated the upland slopes of what is now Gwydyr Forest, incorporating two waymarked forest trails. The route first climbs through the Hafna Mill complex then follows the Conwy Valley View Trail (blue) in reverse to a good viewpoint. Later it descends towards the start which join the waymarked Miners Trail (red) which visits the former Parc mine site, the largest of Gwydyr's lead and zinc mines and other sites hidden in the forest. These abandoned mines now provide an important habitat for hibernating and roosting bats, which are able to access the old underground workings through special open bat-capped shafts. Allow about 2 hours. Also included are the full 2 mile Miners Trail **(Walk B)**, and the 1½ mile Conwy Valley View Trail in reverse **(Walk C)**.

START Hafna Mine car park [SH 781601]

DIRECTIONS From Betws-y-Coed, cross Pont-y-Pair and follow the B5106 north for 3 miles. Just past Gwydir Castle (worth a visit) and immediately before a junction, turn left by a forestry sign and follow a narrow road up the the wooded valley for 1¼ miles to reach the car park on the right.

S *mall-scale mining for lead and zinc began on the Gwydyr estate in the early 17thC, encouraged by its owner, Sir John Wynn, but it was during the 19thC that mining became more organised, employing many men. Fortunes fluctuated and by end of the century, the industry had greatly declined. High mineral prices then saw a revival with some mines re-opening until the 1920s but only Parc, the largest of the Gwydyr mines, continued, until finally closing in the early 1960s.*

The Hafna Mill complex which operated between 1879 – 1915 includes a smelthouse built in the 1880s on the 3rd level. The site also contains the remains of ore bins, sorting, crushing and separation floors, thickening tanks, and a slime pit used to collect residues from the milling process. The prominent chimney was built above the mill to remove toxic fumes formed from smelting. Ore came by an adit and a shaft on the top level.

1 Take the signposted path leading up from the car park entrance to reach the mill complex. (For **Walk B** follow the waymarked Miners Trail up the forestry track to point **2**). Follow the iron railings past the former slime pit to an information board overlooking the car park, then take the railed stepped path up the right hand side of the complex to another information board. Continue up the stepped path passing to the right of the chimney to a stile onto the bend of a stony track. Go up the track and when it bends right follow the waymarked path ahead, then continue up another stony track to a level cross-track. Follow the wide track RIGHT through the forest, then at a track junction bear RIGHT. Shortly the track bears RIGHT again. After about 15 yards, at a green forestry post, a short diversion LEFT on a stony path leads to a picnic table at a viewpoint overlooking the Conwy valley. Continue along the forestry track, past an old track on the left, then an old mine on the right. Soon afterwards the track begins a long steady descent. (For **Walk C**, simply continue down the track to the start.)

2 At a waymarker post by boulders follow the waymarked Miners Trail down through the trees to the road. (*The waymarkers are the traditional mining tools of pick and hammer.*) Continue on the Miners Trail opposite, later alongside a fence to reach a walled area on the site of Parc mine overlooking a side valley. *This area once contained the miners' changing room and shower block. The brown coloured streams below flow from the two main levels of the mine.* Go up the narrow access lane, then on its bend follow the Trail between fences to visit Kneebone's Cutting – *named after Capt. Kneebone, the mine manager when ore was extracted from here.* Return to continue along the lane, then follow the Miners Trail RIGHT up another narrow lane.

3 Soon after passing forestry tracks follow the Miners Trail half-RIGHT to pass the left-hand side of a small building. The Trail continues past a scree slope and the former Parc mine no. 2 level, then descends through trees, past an old building – *formerly office/stores* – then a circular bat-capped shaft to reach a forestry track. Follow it LEFT past further mines hidden in the trees. Later the track bends north towards Hafna Mine. Shortly the Trail turns LEFT off the track up a stony path and continues through the former Vale of Conway Mill site, featuring a crusher house, a circular bat-capped shaft and wheelpit. The path then rises in stages to reach the road. Follow it RIGHT back to the start. (For **Walk B**, shortly follow the waymarked Miners Trail up Tyn yr Ardd's stony access track on the left. Cross a stile on the bend and descend through Hafna mine complex.)

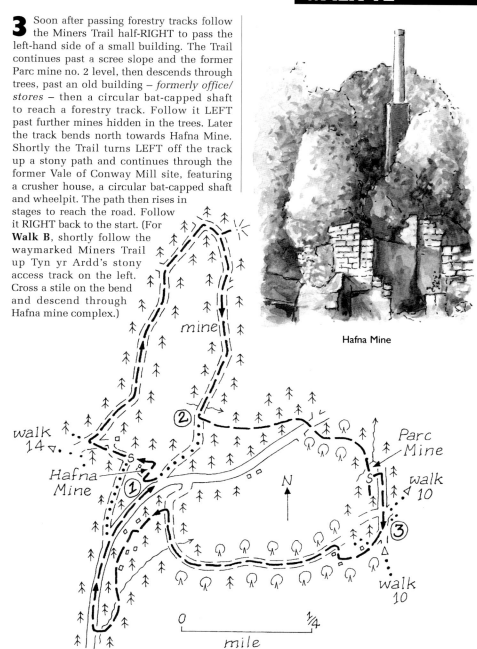

Hafna Mine

WALK 13

SWALLOW FALLS & CYFFTY MINE

DESCRIPTION A choice of a 3½ mile (**A**) or 2½ mile (**B**) walk featuring the Llugwy gorge and the famous Swallow Falls. **Walk A** initially follows the forest trail, before continuing to the Ugly House and following a riverside path to the falls. It then follows woodland and field paths up to the 19thC Cyffty lead-mine, where interpretation panels provide an insight into the old mine workings, and a scenic road back to the start. Allow about 2½ hours. **Walk B** follows a yellow waymarked forest trail through the mixed woodland of Coed Cae Huddygl, steep in places, but featuring a dramatic high viewpoint looking towards Moel Siabod and Snowdon.

START Ty'n Llwyn car park/picnic site [SH 755583]. An alternative start for Walk B is Cyffty mine site [SH 772589].

DIRECTIONS From Betws-y-Coed follow the A5 towards Capel Curig. After crossing the Afon Llugwy take the single-track road on the right alongside the Ugly House and follow the road up the hillside for ¾ mile to reach Ty'n Llwyn car park. The alternative start at Cyffty mine is further along the road.

S *wallow Falls (Rhaeadr-y-Wennol) is perhaps the best known waterfall in North Wales. Its name is actually a mistranslation of its original welsh name of Rhaeadr Ewynol meaning 'foaming cataract'. It is said that the tortured soul of Sir John Wynn of Gwydir who died in 1626, can be heard beneath the lower fall, condemned to remain there after a life of cruelty!*

I From the information board go through a nearby gap in the wall and past picnic tables, then follow the waymarked yellow trail across the open slope and on through trees to a fence gap near a gate adjoining the road. Continue on the wide waymarked yellow trail, soon descending through the wood to a forestry trail board at a path junction. (The path to your left is the returning trail). Keep ahead signposted to Swallow Falls. The trail meanders down through the wood, crosses a wall, then a forestry track, before continuing through the trees down to a forestry track junction. (For **Walk B**, follow the waymarked trail down the lower fork of the track and through the wood. Just after the track becomes a path you reach a path junction. Here bear RIGHT down to a viewpoint overlooking Swallow Falls then continue with Walk A down to point **3**.)

2 For **Walk A** turn RIGHT and follow the track up to a road. Follow it LEFT past The Towers Outdoor Education Centre down to the A5 by the Ugly House (Ty Hyll). *It is said to have originally been a 'ty unnos' – a house built between sunset and sunrise, which according to ancient law gave ownership to the builder if the chimney emitted smoke from a fire by dawn! It is now HQ for the Snowdonia Society.* Turn LEFT towards the bridge to take a signposted path down steps to a ladder-stile to join the Afon Llugwy. Follow the shady riverside path to cross two ladder-stiles, then go along the edge of a field and on through trees to another ladder-stile. Follow the path along the wood edge near the river. Shortly the path splits. The left fork rises to the nearby forestry track where you can rejoin the trail. Preferably continue along the wooded edge of the river to reach a viewpoint overlooking Swallow Falls, where you join Walk B. Continue beside the fence above the river. *Soon a seat below gives a fine view looking back at the falls.* The path now descends above the lower falls through mature trees clinging to the steep slope.

3 Shortly the path splits. For **Walk B** take the waymarked trail left fork up an old forestry track. At a track junction turn LEFT and follow the trail up the narrow track through the wood to reach a stony forestry track. Follow it RIGHT. Shortly the trail, signposted to Ty'n Llwyn car park, rises LEFT from the track up the wooded slope, soon through tall conifers. It later levels out then climbs briefly to a small crag offering a superb viewpoint along the Llugwy valley and to Moel Siabod with Snowdon beyond. Keep away from the edge. Afterwards continue along the waymarked trail, later bearing RIGHT up to join your outward route back to the start.

For **Walk A**, continue ahead down the path and on to cross a footbridge. Follow the path through part-cleared woodland, soon joining an old stony track. After a few yards take the waymarked path angling LEFT off the track, soon bending up through conifers to a finger post and down to a nearby footbridge. Shortly, at a path junction, turn LEFT up the path, and after about 15 yards turn RIGHT up a short path to a road above near a cottage. Take the signposted path opposite alongside the cottage boundary to a stile.

4 Go up the path, then after a few yards turn LEFT to an information panel by a ruin and wheelpit. *The lead-mine, established in the 1850s, was worked from two shafts, with ore being extracted from the Engine*

N

Cyffty mine

Ty'n Llwyn

0 ¼ mile

Coed Cae Huddygl

Ugly House

Afon Llugwy

Swallow Falls

Ugly House

Keep ahead up to a ladder-stile, then follow the path up through mixed woodland, later levelling out and joining a stony cross-path. Follow it RIGHT past a Marin sign. Just beyond, turn sharp LEFT to a stile/gate. Keep ahead to cross a ladder-stile on the right, then angle LEFT across the reedy ground and continue up the field edge, skirting round a wet reedy area, to another ladder-stile into an adjoining field. Angle LEFT up the slope to a waymarker post on the rise ahead and on up to pass the end of a converted stone barn. Follow the nearby house's access track to a ladder-stile/gate. Continue up the track and just before the next stone building angle LEFT across open ground to a ladder-stile. Follow the waymarked path ahead to another ladder-stile at the former Cyffty lead-mine.

Shaft, primarily by horsepower. The wheelpit once housed a 35 ft waterwheel, which originally provided power for pumping water from the mine, then after 1920 helped power a new mineral dressing plant. Buildings below the car parking area date from the 1870s and included a crushing-mill, blacksmiths, and mine office. Continue along the fenced path past another wheelpit to the mine's Western Shaft. Return to the main path and follow it up across a track to the road. Follow it LEFT past the turning for Llyn Geirionydd back to Ty'n Llwyn car park

GWYDYR LAKES

DESCRIPTION A 5½ mile walk (**A**), with extensive views, exploring an area of Gwydyr Forest Park featuring numerous scenic upland lakes that once provided water for the lead-mines. The route first follows a waymarked yellow forest trail in reverse to near Llyn Glangors, then continues down across upland pasture and along the eastern shore of Llyn Geirionydd. After diverting to Llyn Bodgynydd, it then rejoins the forest trail. Allow about 3½ hours. Also included is the full 2½ mile waymarked yellow forest trail in reverse (**B**), and an optional additional ¾ mile walk (**C**) to the 19thC Llanrwst mine engine house and Llyn Sarnau.

START Llyn Sarnau car park [SH 778592].

DIRECTIONS Follow directions in Walk 12 to Hafna mine car park, then continue up the road past Nant-B.H. Outdoor Education Centre to reach a car park on the left by Llyn Sarnau.

I From the information board at the far end of the car park cross the road to the start of the Forest Lakes Walk opposite and follow the yellow trail up into the trees. Soon, when the waymarked trail turns left keep ahead. The path rises steadily, then descends to a stream, and rises again. When it levels out at a path junction bend RIGHT with the waymarked path, briefly descending then continuing through mature woodland. At a waymarked path junction just before a signposted view-point, the trail bends LEFT to a nearby forestry track. Follow it RIGHT.

2 After several bends, turn LEFT off the track past a waymarker post and follow the yellow trail up through a clearing scarred by mining and on to reach another stony for-estry track. Follow it LEFT past a small lake, then turn RIGHT down the trail path and on between the first lake and a larger one. *These attractive lily-covered lakes, a habitat for dragonflies, are known as the Three Dams Reservoir.* The path continues along the larger lake's northern side and on through trees to reach a forestry track. Follow it RIGHT – *soon enjoying a view of Llyn Glangors* – to reach a

waymarker post. (For **Walk B** turn LEFT down the yellow trail towards Llyn Glangors. The path then bends – *now with a view of another lake ahead* – and continues through trees, soon bending down to the end of a forestry track. Follow it past the tree-lined lake and on to seats at point **5**.)

3 About 75 yards further along the track, turn sharp LEFT down a signed path to a ladder-stile near Llyn Glangors. Go across the end of the lake to a stile and up to a telegraph pole. Go down the slope, past another tele-graph pole, to a ladder-stile. Continue ahead, soon passing a further telegraph pole, then descending to a ladder-stile. Continue to a track by the lower of two concrete buildings on the site of the former New Pandora lead mine. Turn RIGHT up the track, then at the second building, turn LEFT to go through a gate in the fence on your right. Continue to a nearby ladder-stile, then follow the path across the part heather covered terrain – *soon with the sight of Llyn Geirionydd below.* The path makes a long steady descent to the lake-side road.

4 Turn LEFT and follow the road along the eastern side of the lake, past a slip-way and car park/toilets. *Llyn Geirionydd is said to be the home of the 6thC poet Talisien. Trees were planted here in 1929 to soften the landscape scarred by intensive mining in the 1870s. The car park stands on the waste tip and the adjacent mine level were part of the New Pandora mine complex. Lead was taken by tramway along the eastern shore of the lake then by aerial ropeway to Klondike lead mill mine 250 feet below.* After passing the end of the lake the road turns up a side valley. Later it passes spoil heaps and a track leading to Ty'n-y-Groes, then a signposted path into a forest. About 40 yards further go across a small parking area on your right to a waymarked Open Access gateway into Cors Bodgynyd Nature Reserve. Follow the stony path past a delightful small lake and an old mine to reach Llyn Bodgynyd – *a reservoir for the Pandora lead-mine.* The path continues along its southern edge. Opposite a tiny island on the wooded shoreline is a seat. Return to the road and take an unsigned path opposite up through mixed woodland to a forestry track where you rejoin the yellow trail. Turn RIGHT past seats at a good viewpoint.

5 Continue along the stony track. Later on a bend at a fenced-off mine and a green forestry post, turn LEFT up an old green track and on to reach another stony forestry track. Follow it RIGHT past a house and at a track junction keep ahead. At another track junction turn LEFT up the track. Just beyond the next bend turn RIGHT on the yellow trail past a waymarker post then take the left fork past another post down to join your outward route.

Walk C From the car park entrance go along the nearby stony forestry track to a ladder-stile on the left. Go up the path, then turn RIGHT to reach a waymarked path junction. Take the left fork to the Llanrwst mine engine house and on to a ladder-stile. Turn RIGHT down the forestry track, then LEFT down an old narrow track opposite a gate/ladder-stile. Shortly, turn RIGHT down a narrow path to join a stony track. Follow it RIGHT past Llyn Sarnau back to the start.

Llyn Bodgynydd

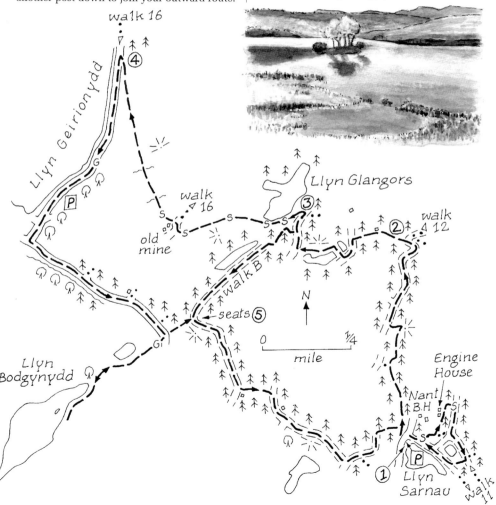

23

LLYN CRAFNANT & LLYN GEIRIONYDD

DESCRIPTION A 5¼ mile walk (**A**) visiting two popular beautiful scenic upland lakes, enclosed by hills and mountains, or an easy 3 mile circuit of Llyn Crafnant (**B**), featuring a seasonal lakeside café. The route follows a waymarked forestry trail along the northern side of Llyn Crafnant and beyond, then joins the valley road. **Walk A** takes a waymarked forestry trail up across a forested ridge and down into the adjoining valley. It then follows a path, uneven in part due to exposed tree roots, along the western side of Llyn Geirionydd, or an equally enjoyable lakeside road alternative, Afterwards it follows a waymarked undulating trail across part-wooded slopes past an old slate mine and down to the start. Allow about 3½ hours. An alternative 2 mile circuit of Llyn Geirionydd can be enjoyed starting from the lakeside car park.
START Crafnant Forestry car park [SH 756618].
DIRECTIONS From the centre of Trefriw, take the road signposted to Llyn Crafnant opposite Gwesty Fairy Falls Hotel. Follow the narrow road up past junctions for nearly 2 miles to reach the car park/toilets.

I From the Gwydyr Forest information board near toilets follow the nearby waymarked yellow trail along the track, then up through trees to the road. Continue up the road above the Afon Crafnant to reach the end of the lake. *Just ahead is a monument erected in 1896 by inhabitants of Llanrwst to commemorate the gift by Richard James of the lake, created into a reservoir for the town.* Turn RIGHT on the waymarked yellow trail across the lake's outlet then follow the stony forestry track along the northern side of the lake. *Llyn Crafnant, ¾ mile long, means 'lake in the valley of garlic'. It contains rainbow and wild brown trout, making it popular with fishermen.* Later keep to the lower waymarked left fork to pass the end of the lake. Shortly, the track becomes a stony path which rises steadily to a waymarked path junction.

2 Here, take the yellow trail left fork down through trees to a ladder-stile. Just below, the path angles LEFT and descends through conifers to cross a footbridge over the stream by Hendre Bach. Turn LEFT, go through a gate and across a stream, then follow the track down beneath a house and on past Tan-y-Manod to join the gated end of the valley road. Follow the narrow road past a house, soon with good views along the lake, then Pen-y-Llyn and Cornel. (For **Walk B** continue along the road past Cynllwyd Mawr, with its lakeside cafe.)

3 At a derelict stone building just before a telephone box, take the waymarked blue trail angling up on the right to a kissing gate and on up the edge of woodland. Just beyond a stream, at a ladder-stile, the blue trail bends sharp RIGHT and rises in stages through conifers. The path eventually levels out and passes through a wall gap, then descends to the bend of a stony forestry track. Keep ahead down the track and at the track junction bend RIGHT. After a few yards, at a blue trail waymarker post, take a path on the left down through trees to rejoin the forestry track. The path continues opposite (if muddy use the track), crosses the track again, and descends to rejoin the forestry track. Follow it down towards Llyn Geirionydd.

4 On the bend cross a stile by a gate ahead. (Alternatively, keep with the track, follow the road alongside the lake, then take a track across its outlet to the monument at point **5**.) Follow the path beneath the cottage then on to the edge of Llyn Geirionydd and a stile at the wood corner. The path keeps close to the wooded edge of the lake, later climbing a small rocky spur above a corner of the lake, before descending near a fence enclosing an old mine to continue along the lakeside. After a stile, keep ahead, then follow a waymarked path alongside a low wall to to reach a track beyond a stone building.

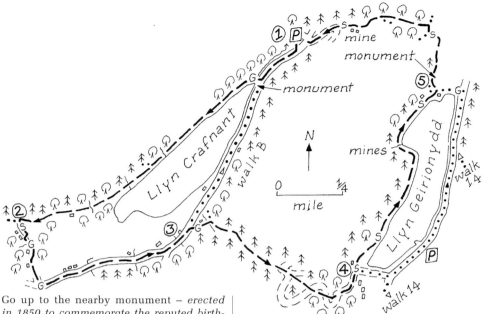

Go up to the nearby monument – *erected in 1850 to commemorate the reputed birth-place of Talisien, a 6thC Chief Bard. It was toppled in a 1976 storm, then re-erected in 1994. In summer, parties of Victorian visitors came here, often entertained by music and sports. Between 1863-1922, an annual poetry/musical event, first established by local poet Gwilym Cowyld, was held at the monument.*

5 Descend its far side to join a wide green path by a Trefriw Trails 5 waymarker post. Follow it past conifers, then angle down through a gap in an old wall. Descend the stony path to a ladder-stile and at a path junction beyond turn RIGHT on the way-marked trail. Soon take the waymarked left fork across the part-wooded slope to a wall-gap. The trail path now rises to a waymarker post at a path junction, where it bears RIGHT and briefly rises before continuing across the part tree and bracken covered hillside to reach an old slate mine site – *which operated from the 18thC until the early 20thC. Continue down the path to the bend of a forestry track and follow it down to the road by the car park.*

Llyn Crafnant monument

WALK 16
LLYN GEIRIONYDD & LLANRHYCHWYN CHURCH

DESCRIPTION A 7 mile walk (**A**) featuring a popular lake above Trefriw and the remote upland Llanrhychwyn church, said to be the oldest in Wales. The route climbs steadily across the part-wooded slopes above Cwm Crafnant, then follows an old tramway to Llyn Geirionydd. After completing a near circuit of the lake via path, uneven in parts due to exposed tree roots, and road, the route rises to a former lead-mine. It then continues to the church or follows an alternative described route past old mines. Allow about 4 hours. Omitting the lake circuit makes an alternative 5¼ mile walk (**B**), whilst the upland country road offers other shorter route options.

START Car park, Trefriw [SH 782630] See Walk 19.

L *lanrhychwyn church, dating from the late 11th/early 12thC, stands on the site of an 'enclosure' (llan), a simple church made of wood or wattle, established in the 6thC by the Celtic saint Rhychwyn. For centuries people have worshipped by candlelight in this charming church, including Llywelyn the Great. Legend says that his wife Joan, daughter of King John of England, despaired of the tiring climb to the church, so in 1230 he had St Mary's church built in Trefriw for her. In the 19thC, this upland parish was extensively worked for lead, zinc and slate, which were shipped from a quay at Trefriw.*

I Return to main road and cross to the woollen mill. Turn RIGHT over the bridge, past shops and a cafe, then turn LEFT up the side road. After 15 yards, take a signposted path on the left, soon above the river. Go past a footbridge and through a kissing gate, then continue under a high footbridge to a seat at Fairy Falls. Follow the path up to a kissing gate, then cross the high footbridge. Turn RIGHT along a path above the river to a road. Turn RIGHT, then at the junction, LEFT up the road. Shortly, take a signposted path on the right (Trefriw Trails 5). Follow the path up through the wood, over a stile, and past a path junction. Follow the waymarked trail across the part wooded slope up to a good viewpoint. Later, after a small gate it crosses a stream and reaches a seat and an information board at a good viewpoint overlooking wooded Cwm Crafnant. *In the valley below is Klondyke Mill (1900-11). Lead and zinc ore was taken by tramway along Llyn Geirionydd's eastern shore from the New Pandora mine, then by aerial ropeway from here to the mill 250 feet below for processing.* Continue along the former tramway, crossing two ladder-stiles to reach the road. (For **Walk B** continue along the road to point 3.)

2 Just before the lake go through a kissing gate and follow a track across its outlet. *The monument ahead was originally erected in 1850 to commemorate the reputed birthplace of Taliesen, a 6thC Chief Bard.* Just past a stone building, turn LEFT to follow a path alongside a wall down to the lake. Continue on the lakeside path, past old mines, across a small spur and on through conifers, then a meadow to reach a forestry track near a cottage. Follow it LEFT to a road. Turn LEFT and follow the lakeside road past the car park/toilets.

3 Later, at a gate across the road at a forest corner, take the signposted path on the right back up across the hillside. After a ladder-stile turn LEFT, then go through a gate on your right. Turn LEFT alongside the fence past the site of the former New Pandora lead mine to reach a track. Follow it LEFT through a gate and up to Castell-y-Gwynt, then the stiled path past the house. Continue alongside its garden wall and on up to go through a gate – *with a view of Llyn Glangors.*

4 Here you have a choice. (For the ***mines route*** keep ahead, and after 50 yards angle RIGHT to follow a path near the boundary to cross a stile into the forest. The stiled path follows the forest edge, then descends past mines and spoiltips to eventually reach a forestry track. Follow it LEFT to Tan-yr-Eglwys farm. Continue from paragraph 5.) For the **church route** angle LEFT up the slope, soon passing a reedy area to reach a rise – *with extensive mountain views*. Go down alongside an old wall, past a small ruin and on to a ladder-stile/gate. Keep ahead, soon bearing half-LEFT down a wide path and through a reedy area, then descending again between two small grassy ridges to a ladder-stile in the wall below. The path descends through trees to a ladder-stile, then continues to a gate by cottages. Go along their access track. On the bend go through a kissing gate ahead to nearby Llanrhychwyn church. From the lychgate follow the fence down to a kissing gate (Trefriw Trails 8). Go down the field to another kissing gate by Ty'n-y-coed, then over its access track down to a further kissing gate. Continue down to a small gate onto a track by Tan-yr-Eglwys farm. Turn LEFT.

5 Follow the access track, then road to crossroads by houses. Go along the road ahead, later descending steeply to the outskirts of Trefriw. Just before Y Wern and your outward path, take the signposted enclosed stony path on your right down to a road, which you follow down to a junction. Follow the road RIGHT down to the main road by the school. Turn LEFT.

Llanrhychwyn Church

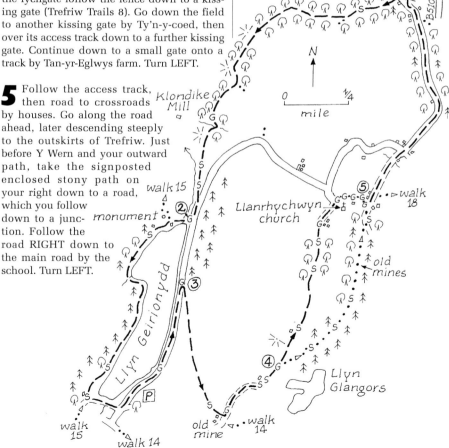

WALK 17

LLANRWST – TREFRIW

DESCRIPTION A 4¾ mile figure of eight level walk between two historic communities, partly along the Conwy and Crafnant rivers. Allow about 2½ hours. The route can be undertaken as a 3 mile walk from Trefriw or a 1¾ mile walk from Llanrwst.

START Plas yn Dre car park, Llanrwst [SH 796618] or car park, Trefriw [SH 782630].

DIRECTIONS The car park, near the library and police station, is signposted off the A470 just north of Llanrwst centre. See Walk 19 for the alternative Trefriw start.

*L*lanrwst *is an ancient market town known for the making of harps and clocks, and in the 19thC, the spinning of woollen yarn and the knitting of stockings. Pont Mawr was designed by the famous architect Indigo Jones and built in 1636, at an expense of £1,000 shared jointly by Caernarvon and Denbigh counties. Nearby Gwydir Castle, dating from the 16thC, was the seat of the influential Wynn family.*

1 Return to the main road and follow it LEFT. Shortly go along Station Road, then just before North Llanrwst railway station follow a road LEFT to a pedestrian suspension bridge over the Afon Conwy. *This is a mid-20thC replacement for the original wooden Gower's Bridge, named after the Rev. John Gower, who also built the lane ahead in the 1880s to provide a link, financed by tolls levied, between Trefriw and Llanrwst railway station. Fishing was popular with Victorian visitors, and coracles were a common sight on the river.* Cross the bridge then a stile on the right and follow the path north along the top of the flood embankment, later leaving the Afon Conwy and heading south alongside the Afon Crafnant towards Trefriw. Go past a footbridge, through a kissing gate and briefly along a track, before following an enclosed riverside path to toilets and a minor road below Trefriw woollen mill.

2 Follow the road LEFT past the car parking area then enter the Recreation Ground. Follow a path through a children's playground and over a grass embankment then bear RIGHT along a wide path to a gate. Keep ahead, soon on a narrow path parallel with the adjoining lane, later joining it to reach the suspension bridge. Cross the stile on the right and follow the path along the embankment, then cross a stile on the left and a watercourse. Follow the stiled path through four fields, then a hedge-lined green track to the road by Tu Hwnt I'r Bont. Cross Pont Mawr, then follow a riverside path back to the car park

WALK 18

GRINLLWM

DESCRIPTION An 8 mile walk of great variety exploring the Conwy valley and its part-wooded edges between Llanrwst and Trefriw, featuring gentle riverside walking, two waterfalls, a short steep climb to the outlying hill of Grinllwm (942 feet/287 metres) with good views, and the remote ancient Llanrhychwyn church (See Walk 16 for information). Allow about 4½ hours. An alternative shorter return route is shown.

START As Walk 17.

1 Follow instructions in section **1** of **Walk 17** to Trefriw.

2 Join the main road by the woollen mill. Turn RIGHT across the bridge, past shops and a cafe, then turn LEFT up the side road. After 15 yards, take a signposted path on the left, soon above the river. Go past a footbridge, through a kissing gate and on under a high footbridge to a seat at Fairy Falls. Follow the path up to a kissing gate, then cross the high footbridge and follow the walled path ahead to a road. Go up Jubilee Road opposite, then on the bend follow the waymarked enclosed path up to a road. Turn RIGHT past Y Wern, then take a signposted path (Trefriw Trails 5) on the left. It rises steadily through woodland to a stile. About 100 yards further, at a Trails 5 waymarker post, take a minor path angling LEFT up the wooded slope. After a more open aspect, it rises more steeply, briefly near a wall on your right, up the now bracken-covered slope to a ladder-stile onto Grinllwm's Open Access land. Continue alongside the old fence to a gate in it.

3 Here you have a choice. A simple option is to continue with the fence down to a lane. A better alternative is to head LEFT up Grinllwm to its craggy top for all-round views. Go to another nearby top for a view down to Llanrwst, then descend south to join a good path about 20 yards above a wall, which it follows down to a lane. Follow it LEFT to a road junction. Turn RIGHT and at the next junction keep ahead. On the bend go through a kissing gate to nearby Llanrhychwyn church. From the lych-gate follow the fence down to a kissing gate. Go down the field to another kissing gate by Ty'n-y-coed, then descend to a further kiss-ing gate. Continue down to a track at Tan-yr-Eglwys farm. Turn LEFT.

4 Just beyond outbuildings go through a gate set back on the right. Follow a green track through another gate, over a stream in trees to a stile/gate. Go ahead across the field to a stile/gate, then follow a track through a wood to another stile/gate. Keep ahead down to a ladder-stile and a narrow road below. Turn RIGHT down the road past a signposted path (an alternative return route). After a further ½ mile you pass a ladder-stile giving access to the Grey Mare's Tail waterfall.

5 At a junction go along the track oppo-site, taking its right fork through the Saw

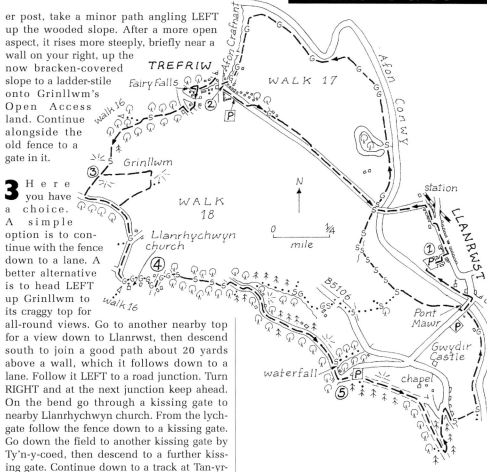

Bench forestry car park. Go past the Marin mountain bike trail information board and the barrier gate ahead. Continue along the stony track on the yellow/white walks trails. Shortly, keep on the higher right fork (yellow trail). After ¼ mile at a waymarker post turn sharp LEFT down a public footpath through the forest to a road, which you follow down to the B5106. Turn RIGHT along the grass verge opposite. Shortly cross a ladder-stile and go down the field edge, then follow the riverside path to the road by Tuhwnt I'r Bont tearooms and Pont Mawr. Cross the bridge and follow the riverside path back to the car park.

WALK 19

COED CREIGIAU

DESCRIPTION A waymarked 2¼ mile woodland circuit of Coed Cregiau above Trefriw. Allow about 1½ hours.
START Car park, Trefriw [SH 782630].
DIRECTIONS A minor road opposite Trefriw woollen mill leads to a car parking area.

Until the arrival of the railway 1860s, Trefriw was an important inland port serving the valley. In the first half of the 19thC, vessels carried coal, lime and general goods up the river, and returned tull of slate, lead ore and timber from the surrounding hills. It was also an important cloth-weaving centre. A fulling mill, taking woven cloth from cottages to wash and finish, was established in 1820. It then developed into the woollen mill, whose products are as popular today as in Victorian/Edwardian times when Trefriw became a fashionable spa resort. The curative properties of the sulphor and iron-rich waters of the chalybeate wells to the north of the village, known since Roman times, attracted many visitors. Passenger steamer services ran until World War II – at their peak bringing up to 1000 people a day along the river. Of various industries once dependent on the river Crafnant, including a cornmill, sawmill, and forge which made hammers/chisels for the slate quarries, only the woollen mill survives.

1 Return to main road and cross to the woollen mill. Go over the nearby bridge, past shops and a cafe, then turn LEFT up a road. Follow it up past side roads, then turn RIGHT up a road signposted to the cemetery and Llyn Cowlyd. Shortly, turn RIGHT up a track on a waymarked 'Trefriw Trails 6' path into Coed Creigiau, an area of mixed woodland. When it splits take the waymarked right fork. Shortly, the trail turns LEFT off the track and rises through conifers, soon following a cross-path right up to a stony forestry track. Follow it RIGHT up to a track junction, then turn sharp LEFT up the other track. After about 150 yards follow a green track angling LEFT off the track to a seat at

a good viewpoint. About 100 yards further take a wide path on the right up to rejoin the forestry track. Follow it LEFT, soon descending to the edge of Coed Creigiau.

2 Just before the barrier gate and a road look for a trail waymarker on a tree to the left. Follow the trail down the edge of the wood, soon just above the road. On its bend, the waymarked trail continues through tall pines, then turns RIGHT down a wide cross-path to join a stony track. Follow it RIGHT to rejoin your outward route.

WALK 20

CEFN CYFARWYDD

DESCRIPTION An exhilarating 8 mile walk for experienced hill walkers, exploring a little known upland area north west of Trefriw. The route first follows a waymarked trail through Coed Cregiau, then rises in stages along a scenic upland road, before heading along the edge of Cwm Ddu past a remote ruined chapel and abandoned upland farms, requiring careful navigation over occasionally wet reedy terrain. It then follows the narrow Llyn Cowlyd access road over Cefn Cyfarwydd, reaching a height of 1410 feet/430 metres, for a dramatic descent with breathtaking views. Allow about 4½ hours. Avoid in poor visibility.
START Car park, Trefriw [SH 782630].

1 Follow instructions in paragraph **1** of **Walk 19**.

2 After leaving Coed Creigiau continue up the attractive narrow road, then at a junction turn RIGHT. Follow the delightful scenic upland road offering extensive views, later rising in stages and passing two houses. It then descends to a large modern house and continues down towards farm buildings. Go through the left of two gateways ahead to pass between a part red-bricked barn and a large corrugated shed. Continue along a gated track through a small wood, then past a graveyard and ruined Calvinist Methodist chapel – *established in the mid-19thC to serve the scattered upland Welsh-speaking community* – and on to cross an old leat to reach an abandoned upland farm. Go past the left-hand side of the buildings (gates).

3 Follow a green track beside the fence, over a stream and along the field edge to old gates near a stone barn. Continue ahead up the old reedy track. When it fades keep ahead up through reedy ground to a good viewpoint looking ahead along the valley. Follow the remains of a boulder wall on your right past a tree, then a path across the gorse covered terrain. Soon join a quad track which crosses reedy tussocky terrain, then becomes a path as it passes through more gorse to a gate in a fence. Go down the wettish ground to pass just to the left of the small tree-covered rocky knoll ahead, then follow an old boulder wall to a waymarker post by a stream just beyond its corner. After a further 15 yards, angle LEFT

4 Just before the wall corner the path angles LEFT to pass to the left of trees ahead, then angles RIGHT through reeds to pass an enclosed old ruined cottage amongst Scots pines. Continue towards a more substantial ruined house ahead, then pass to the right of its outbuilding. Work your way across the reedy ground, then follow the old fence on your left to where it crosses a large old walled enclosure. Turn LEFT alongside the old wall and round to its far corner then continue ahead down tussocky ground. Just before an old embanked boundary with a fence beyond head LEFT to a ladder-stile. Go up the slope ahead to pass just to the right of a tree, and on past the end of a walled enclosure. Continue to a small slab bridge over a stream and a gate by a ruin to reach the hidden road just above. (For Llyn Cowlyd, turn right.) Follow it LEFT on a long steady climb to pass over Cefn Cyfarwydd ridge to enjoy dramatic mountain and valley views. As you descend, Llyn Geirionydd comes into view. Eventually you rejoin your outward route. Follow the road down past Coed Creigiau and the cemetery into Trefriw.

Cwm Ddu

leat

old chapel

N

③

ruin

④
ruins

Cefn Cyfarwydd

0 — ¼
mile

Walk 20

ruins

Coed Creigiau

Walk 19

②

Cemetery

TREFRIW

walks 16 & 18

woollen mill

① P

up a cross-path. At a small stone ruin, ignore the path angling left past it, but keep ahead to cross a nearby stream by trees. After a few yards angle LEFT up a path and across reedy ground to pass just to the right of rock covered high ground ahead. Continue through reeds, passing to the left of a tree, then the nearby wall of a large enclosure.

WALK 21
PORTH-LLWYD FALLS

DESCRIPTION A demanding but interesting 3 mile walk ascending the steep hidden wooded slopes above Dolgarrog, returning past Porth-llwyd waterfall, popular with Victorian visitors, then incorporating an optional short informative waymarked trail commemorating the worst dam disaster in Welsh history. On 2nd November 1925 the dam of Llyn Eigiau, which supplied power to generate electricity, was breached, and water cascaded down the hillside destroying part of Dolgarrog and killing 16 people. Allow about 2 hours. It links to Walk 22 offering an easy ½ mile extension to Coedty reservoir.

START Dolgarrog [SH 769677].

DIRECTIONS Park in a side road just off the B5106 opposite the Dolgarrog and District Social Club.

behind another house, take a signposted path on the left. It rises across the wooded slope to join another path just below a house. Pass between the house and outbuilding, then follow a meandering enclosed path up through trees, past a path on the right, to a waymarked tree just before a ladder-stile. Follow the path bearing RIGHT, soon bending LEFT. Continue up the enclosed woodland path – *once a highway* – passing two ruins. It then bends across the wooded slope beside an old wall and rises steadily past a walled path on the right and a small ruin to the entrance to Llidiart Fadog. Follow the narrow lane for ½ mile past a farm entrance up to a minor road. Turn LEFT up the road over a leat. Later, after crossing the leat again, the road descends.

2 On a bend, take a signposted path over a ladder-stile on the left (or first continue to Pont Newydd or Coedty reservoir). Follow the fence on your right above the wooded valley, shortly crossing an old wall and descending to a ladder-stile. Follow

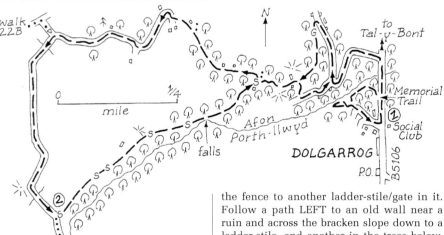

the fence to another ladder-stile/gate in it. Follow a path LEFT to an old wall near a ruin and across the bracken slope down to a ladder-stile, and another in the trees below. The path now descends the wooded gorge past Porth-llwyd waterfall, then bends away and gradually descends to a ladder-stile to join your outward route. At the path junction below the house, take the path bearing RIGHT down to a lane. Follow it LEFT down to Ceunant and return along your outward route, then follow the memorial trail, returning down a lane to the side road.

1 Walk north along the B5106 past the start of the memorial trail, then turn LEFT up a narrow no through road, soon enclosed by woodland. Shortly the road bends right past Ceunant, a pottery, by a side road. When

WALK 22
CWM PORTH-LLWYD

DESCRIPTION A 5½ mile (**A**) or 7 mile (**B**) walk, with extensive views, exploring remote upland valleys crossed by leats, water pipes, and former narrow gauge railways used in the construction of several reservoir dams. From a high start (820 feet) the route follows a former railway past Coedty reservoir and along the edge of Cwm Porth-llwyd. **Walk A** then crosses Moel Eilio ridge at 1509 feet/460 metres and returns along the upper edge of Cwm Ddu. **Walk B** continues to Llyn Eigiau then returns via track and scenic upland roads. It provides an easier walk among open mountain scenery and can be started or varied from an alternative upland car park. Allow about 3½ hours. Both walks combine well with Walk 21 for a Dolgarrog start.

START Pont Newydd [SH759671] or car park near Llyn Eigiau [SH 732663].

DIRECTIONS In Tal-y-Bont, turn off the B5106 on a minor road near the school. It rises steeply through sharp bends to a junction after 1 mile. (For the alternative car park follow the road ahead for a further 2 miles.) Turn left for ½ mile to find limited parking just beyond Pont Newydd or near the road end.

Continue up the road, under a pipeline and up to cross a leat, where the road becomes two tracks. Bear RIGHT through a nearby gate and follow a track past Coedty reservoir, through woodland and over a leat to a ladder-stile/gate. The delightful green track continues up and across the expansive Cwm Porth-llwyd beneath Moel Eilio. *This former 2ft gauge railway, which followed the route of a 19th C slate tramway connecting Cedryn quarry with an incline through Coed Dolgarrog, operated between 1907-1910 during the*

building of Llyn Eigiau dam, its walls now visible ahead. Its lower section was used in the building of Coedty dam in 1924. After a choice of tracks crossing a stream you go through a gate.

2 Shortly, for **Walk A** cross a ladder-stile on the left. (For **Walk B** cross a ladder-stile ahead and follow the track to Llyn Eigiau, then another past the dam, across its outlet and along the valley to the car park. Follow the road, past an alternative path option, to the junction. Turn right back to the start.) Follow the old green track up the hillside and on past an abandoned cottage to cross a stream and ladder-stile. The path rises to another ladder-stile, then crosses the slope before passing over the shoulder of Moel Eilio. Here the path splits. Take the LEFT fork. It steadily descends – *with a view of Llyn Cowlyd* – to a ladder-stile. Follow the fence LEFT down to a gate and ladder-stile just above the pipeline. Descend through bracken for a few yards, then follow a path LEFT soon rising to cross a stream at a wall/fence corner. Follow the path up to pass to the left of a ruin and across reedy/tussocky terrain, becoming a narrow green track and passing another ruin.

After a ladder-stile/gate, continue on the old green track (*reputedly a Roman road*), shortly rising and bending to a ladder-stile/gate, then beginning a long steady descent to join your outward route.

33

PEN-Y-GAER, LLYN DULYN & LLYN MELYNLLYN

DESCRIPTION An exhilarating 10 mile figure of eight walk, with extensive views, from Pen-y-gaer Iron Age hillfort across a wild remote upland valley to lakes, used as reservoirs, set in two of the most dramatic corries in Snowdonia, beneath the central Carneddau mountain ridge. After visiting the hillfort, the route follows a delightful track to cross the Afon Ddu, after which mainly level paths across wettish ground take you to Llyn Dulyn, where there is a bothy nearby for shelter. A short steep climb to Llyn Melynllyn, at 2,099 feet/640 metres, is followed by a scenic high-level track, then another takes you to a small dam, after which you follow paths, later well waymarked. The route follows existing rights of way and a few well used link paths across Open Access land. Although, the walk starts slow and involves little demanding climbing, it is for experienced hill walkers only, and should be avoided in poor visibility. Allow between 5-6 hours. The route can be shortened to a 5 mile walk (**B**). Another option is a 5¾ mile walk (**C**) around Cwm Melynllyn to the lakes from the alternative upland car park also accessed from Tal-y-Bont (See Walk 22).

START Pen-y-gaer [SH 744693] or car park, near Llyn Eigiau [SH 732663].

DIRECTIONS From the Bedol pub in Tal-y-Bont, take the road signposted to Llanbedr-y-cennin. Go past Ye Olde Bull Inn and continue up the hillside, enjoying extensive views. At a junction, turn left and follow the road up below the northern slopes of Pen-y-Gaer to its end, where it becomes two tracks and there is a parking area.

| From the road end take the track leading south to cross a ladder-stile on the left. A clear path takes you to another ladder-stile providing access to the hillfort. Its defences included the rare 'cheveux de frise' – *angled pointed stones embedded in the ground.* Retrace your steps, then follow the other track, soon rising to cross an old leat and a ladder-stile. Follow the track rising gently alongside the wall beneath Penygadair, over another ladder-stile, and past one on your left (your return route). The track continues across the open slopes up to another ladder-stile, then rises steadily past another ladder-stile, where it levels out, and begins a long steady descent. *Ahead in the distance, below the Carneddau ridge, are the imposing dark crags, beneath which are the hidden lakes you seek.* After a ladder-stile, continue ahead on the now faint green track, shortly beginning another long descent. Later the track fades again as it passes through a wet area to a ladder-stile just before the Afon Ddu.

2 After crossing the river, turn LEFT and work your way across wettish ground above the river alongside the fence, which later becomes a wall, to an iron ladder-stile. (For **Walk B**, cross it and resume text at point **5**.) Here, turn RIGHT to follow a path SW along the edge of a line of rushes to cross a footbridge. Continue ahead to cross an iron ladder-stile in a fence. Ultimately you are aiming to pass to the right of a small group of trees ahead. In the meanwhile, continue ahead guided by occasional small concrete 'cable below' posts. Cross a stream, then another by an old stone sheepfold and continue to a ladder-stile. Keep ahead for about 150 yards, first passing above large boulders, then over two small streams. Now bear LEFT to cross a larger stream coming from the high ground ahead and go across a shoulder into Cwm Melynllyn to join a good path passing above the Scots pines. Follow it along the valley edge to pass above Dulyn bothy to reach Llyn Dulyn. *Lying beneath the near vertical crags of Craig y Dulyn, which have claimed the lives of airmen, this dark lake is said to be 189 ft deep.*

3 Cross the outlet and end of the lake to join a embanked path below where piped water from Llyn Melynllyn falls to be channelled into the lake, and continue on the path angling up the hillside on the line of the hidden pipeline, to eventually cross a small footbridge at the NE corner of Llyn Melynllyn. From here, a track just out of sight, heads SE, to pass a ruined building. *The remains*

Penygadair

Pen·y·gaer

footbridge

Afon Ddu

Afon Melynllyn

N

0   ¼

mile

walk 22

then follow a clear path, initially above the river, soon rising to follow a wall up to cross the iron ladder-stile met on the outward route.

5 Cross the nearby footbridge, then follow a path contouring across the boulder-covered slope, later guided by occasional concrete posts, to cross an iron ladder-stile. The path crosses a stream, briefly runs alongside a wall, then follows a series of waymarker posts to another iron ladder-stile. Continue ahead. After a wall gap, the waymarked path angles LEFT up to go through another wall-gap and on to pass a ruined hafod. At the end of a walled section, the path rises LEFT and meanders across the hillside guided by waymarker posts to eventually reach a wall/fence corner. Follow the fence to a ladder-stile, where you rejoin your outward route.

of a wheelpit and old machinery are associated with the former Melynllyn slate quarry (1867-1908) on the slopes beyond. The track – the former tramway serving the quarry – continues across the mid-slopes, offering good views of your outward route. After a while it begins a long steady descent via two ladder-stiles, then levels out, before meandering down towards the adjoining expansive valley, with a good view of Llyn Eigiau. Just before a ladder-stile/ gate, turn sharp LEFT onto another track.

4 Follow the track down to cross a small dam over the Afon Melynllyn. Bear LEFT over the Afon Ddu to cross a ladder-stile (For **Walk C** follow a path heading half-left, rising steadily across open ground to join the main route at the footbridge) Continue ahead passing above the nearby building,

Llyn Dulyn

ROWEN TO LLANBEDR-Y-CENNIN

DESCRIPTION A 6 mile walk exploring the attractive contrasting undulating countryside between two attractive villages with delightful traditional inns. The route follows field paths and quiet lanes to the foot Pen-y-Gaer, offering an optional extension up to its Iron Age hillfort. After crossing its eastern slopes, reaching a height of 984 feet/300 metres and offering good views of the Conwy valley, the route passes below an upland leat, then descends old tracks to reach Llanbedr-y-Cennin, with its medieval church and Ye Olde Bull Inn. The return includes a section of delightful riverside walking. Allow about 3½ hours.

START Rowen [SH 761719].

DIRECTIONS Rowen is signposted from the B5106. There is roadside parking near the first houses

Rowen stands on an ancient highway, which later formed part of the Roman road from nearby Canovium to Segontium (Caernarfon), and was subsequently used by drovers and travellers. The upland landscape above the village is rich in monuments and sites of early settlers, including standing stones, burial chambers and hillforts. Rowen once had several mills and inns, but only the Ty Gwyn remains.

1 Continue into the village, then just before the Ty Gwyn Hotel, cross a footbridge over the river. Go past Pen y Bont and through a gate ahead, then follow a delightful old walled green track/path to an old farm. Angle RIGHT past the end of the building and follow the enclosed path to an iron ladder-stile/gate. Head across the field up to another ladder-stile/gate. Go up the green track, then just before a gate and ladder-stile, turn RIGHT and follow the boundary up the field edge and round to a ladder-stile in the corner. Follow the enclosed path down to

cross a ladder-stile near a house Turn RIGHT along the field edge, through a gateway ahead then cross a ladder-stile on the right. Continue to another ladder-stile ahead, then turn LEFT up a track through trees to its end at a facing gate.

2 Follow the fence on your left above an old sunken walled path up the edge of three fields to an iron ladder-stile. Continue along the edge of the next two fields to a ladder-stile in a wall ahead. Follow a path ahead through a large area of rough pasture, later joining another old sunken path on the left to reach a ladder-stile/gateway in the corner. Follow the enclosed path to a nearby minor road. Follow it LEFT, then turn RIGHT between an outbuilding and the gated entrance to Waen Isa to cross a stone stile by a gate. Angle LEFT up to a gate, and follow a path ahead passing to the right of a nearby large pylon. After an area of gorse go through a gap in an old wall and continue across the large field past a telegraph post to a ladder-stile/gate onto a minor road. Follow it LEFT, then at a junction turn RIGHT and continue up the road.

3 On the bend beneath Pen-y Gaer take the signposted path on the left. (To visit the hillfort, an Open Access area, continue up the road for 30 yards, take a signposted path up to a ladder-stile, then angle right up the steep gorse-covered hillside to a wall and follow it up to a ladder-stile and a path leading to the fort.) Go through two gates by an old farm and continue beside the wall. As it begins to descend angle RIGHT across the bracken covered ground beneath gorse to join another wall. Follow it up to cross a ladder-stile in it. Turn RIGHT and follow a path up to another ladder-stile. Follow the path across the hillside then angle LEFT down to cross a ladder-stile in a wall. Walk beneath an embankment supporting a leat above, and as it bends away, continue to a ladder-stile/gate ahead. Go through a bracken covered field, soon angling down to cross a ladder-stile/gate in the bottom left-hand corner.

4 Turn LEFT to follow a delightful enclosed green track meandering steadily down the part-wooded hillside, passing through a gate and continuing down to a junction of tracks by outbuildings. Turn RIGHT and follow the access track down to pass Cae Asaph, then bend sharp LEFT past an outbuilding and continue down a narrow track to a gate. Just beyond turn LEFT along a hedge-lined track, soon descending steeply to join an access lane by cottages. Follow it LEFT to a junction. Turn RIGHT down the road into Llanbedr-y-cennin to reach the junction by the Ye Olde Bull Inn – a tempting refreshment stop! *The village lies on a drovers route across the Carneddau mountains and is known for Ffynnon Bedr, a holy well said to have curative properties.* Turn LEFT up the road past St Peter's medieval church (*worth a visit*) then a side road. Continue down the road. On the bend by Cennin Cottage go through the gate ahead and follow the signposted path along a track past Primrose Bank Cottage to cross a ladder-stile.

5 Follow the boundary on your left down to a ladder-stile, and go down the next field edge to cross another ladder-stile on the right just before a house. Descend through trees to a gate and go past the end of a large farm outbuildings. Turn LEFT along the side of the lower one to a gate, then keep ahead to a ladder-stile by the river. Cross the farm's access lane and the stile opposite. Now follow the stiled riverside path through three fields, then angle away from the river past a small wood and up to a ladder-stile in the top field corner onto a road. Follow it RIGHT over the river to a junction in the small hamlet of Pontwgan. Turn LEFT along the road, soon crossing the river. Just before another bridge over the

Ty Gwyn

river, take a signposted path through a kissing gate on the left. Walk along the edge of the long and narrowing field by the river to a ladder-stile. Bear LEFT across the next field to join your outward route at the old farm. Follow it back to Rowen and the hospitality

WALK 25

ST CELYNIN'S CHURCH & TAL Y FAN

DESCRIPTION A choice of routes exploring a fascinating scenic upland landscape, full of antiquity, featuring a remote ancient church, Maen Penddu and other standing stones, an ancient burial chamber, hillfort, a section of Roman road, combined with panoramic views. The main 7 mile walk (**A**) includes an exhilarating climb along the ridge of Taly y Fan, at just under 2000 feet, Snowdonia's most northerly mountain. Although not a difficult ascent, this is for experienced walkers and should be avoided in poor visibility. Allow about 5 hours. Lower level alternative 5½ mile (**B**) and 6½ mile (**C**) walks are included.
START Rowen [SH 761719].
DIRECTIONS See Walk 24.

I Walk through the village past the Ty Gwyn Hotel, attractive stone houses and a chapel. On the bend turn RIGHT on a signposted path along a lane to a farm. Go through the gate ahead, down the field to the bottom left-hand corner to cross a ladder-stile beyond. Turn RIGHT along a stony track and on the bend cross a ladder-stile ahead. Go along the field edge to another ladder-stile, then follow the raised path up alongside a fence to a narrow road. Follow it RIGHT, then take a signposted path up an access lane on the left past Lwynonn. Later as bends right to a farm cross a ladder-stile ahead. Go along the right-hand bank of the stream, then cross it and follow the wall on your left up to a waymarked gate in it. Turn RIGHT over the stream then head across to Dodre'r coed cottage. At its entrance turn LEFT up a track, soon bearing RIGHT to a gate above the cottage. The track now rises steadily up the open, then part-wooded hillside. After a small stream, the track bends left then right. About 70 yards further, follow a waymarked path angling RIGHT to cross a nearby ladder-stile/stream and up the tree-covered slope into a field. Continue up to a gate between an outbuilding and a ruined cottage. Pass behind the ruin and go up a path.

2 After about 10 yards, the route turns sharp LEFT past a hawthorn tree. (First follow the wide path ahead to a nearby superb viewpoint.) Follow the improving path up beneath bracken and gorse, then beside a wall up to a ladder-stile. Go along the left-hand side of the small ridge ahead, then across a reedy area, and past another small ridge, with a ruin to your left. Continue along the field, with the church now visible, to a ladder-stile in the top left-hand corner. Go along a green track, then at track junction turn RIGHT to reach the church entrance. *St Celynin's church is a delightful simple building, whose nave dates from the 14thC. Summer services and harvest thanksgiving are still held here. In the south corner of the churchyard is a rectangular well, renowned for its power to heal sick children. Near the churchyard gate once stood an inn which served travellers crossing the mountains.* Return along the track and past a ladder-stile. When it bends right go through a gate ahead and follow a narrow green track up past a nearby house – *soon with a view of Tal-y-fan ahead* – to a gate into Open Access land by sheepfolds. Go through another gate ahead and follow the green track across open country.

3 After about 150 yards as the track rises half-left you have a choice:
For **Walk B** continue up the green track curving round the western side of Craig Celynin. About midway, the track bears half-RIGHT, rising gently, then after a stream becomes a path, which continues alongside the wall ahead. After passing a small triangular enclosure, bear RIGHT – *the mound on your right is Caer Bach, a 1st millennium BC hillfort* – and follow the old wall on your left up to a gate. Keep alongside the wall to cross two ladder-stiles, then follow the main path, later rejoining the wall to cross another ladder-stile. Follow the green track down to go through two gates below Cae Coch, then cross a ladder-stile onto a track. Turn LEFT and resume instructions at paragraph **5**.

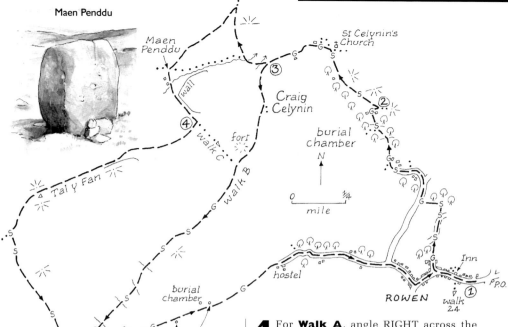

Maen Penddu

St Celynin's Church

Maen Penddu

Craig Celynin

burial chamber

fort

Tal y Fan

burial chamber

standing stones

hostel

Inn

ROWEN

walk 2.4

P.O.

N

0   ¼   mile

For **Walk A** take a path angling away on the right through heather and gorse to cross a stream between two wall corners. Take the path close by the wall on your right - (the other is an alternative route to Maen Penddu as shown.) Follow it across open upland pasture, later turning sharp LEFT up a green track across the gorse-covered pasture towards Tal y Fan, to reach Maen Penddu. *This large flat-topped stone, almost 2 metres high, and an almost buried stone circle nearby, date from the 2nd millennium BC and were likely of ceremonial importance.* Here, turn LEFT and follow a path to cross a stream by the second of two ruins. The path now rises and continues alongside a wall. As the wall begins to gently curve follow a path straight ahead. After about 100 yards the ground begins to descend. (For **Walk C** continue ahead down the slope to join Walk B at the old wall near Cae Bach hillfort.)

4 For **Walk A**, angle RIGHT across the boulder-covered slope to join a well-used path heading directly up the mountain, about 100 yards from a ruin to your left. At the top of the slope, the path briefly bears right, then continues across a depression on the NE side of the mountain before rising to the wall on the Tal y Fan ridge. A good path follows the wall west along the undulating rocky ridge, past a ladder-stile accessing the summit trig point, then shortly begins a long initially steep descent to cross a ladder-stile at the bwlch. Now follow the occasionally waymarked, stiled path down the southern slopes of Tal y Fan to a road. Turn LEFT and on the bend continue ahead along a track to the entrance to Cae Coch.

5 Now follow the old enclosed green lane, soon on a steady descent, to reach the Youth Hostel, then continue down the steep road into Rowen. *The lane is an ancient route, which later became part of the Roman road from Canovium fort in the Conwy valley to Segontium fort at Caernarfon. On the adjoining slopes are 2nd millennium BC standing stones and Maen y Bard Neolithic burial chamber.*

39

PRONUNCIATION

These basic points should help non-Welsh speakers

Welsh	English equivalent
c	always hard, as in cat
ch	as on the Scottish word loch
dd	as th in then
f	as in of
ff	as in off
g	always hard as in got
ll	no real equivalent. It is like 'th' in then, but with an 'L' sound added to it, giving 'thlan' for the pronunciation of the Welsh 'Llan'.

In Welsh the accent usually falls on the last-but-one syllable of a word.

KEY TO THE MAPS

- ➜ Walk route and direction
- ══ Metalled road
- ‑‑‑ Unsurfaced road
- •••• Footpath/route adjoining walk route
- ∿➔ River/stream
- ⋆ ۞ Trees
- ▬▬ Railway
- **G** Gate
- **S** Stile
- ⛌ Viewpoint
- Ⓟ Parking
- Ⓣ Telephone

Useful contacts

Conwy County Borough Council 01492 574000 or www.conwy gov.uk for reporting RoW problems
www.forestry.gov.uk/gwydyrforestpark for reporting path problems in Gwydyr Forest Park
traveline 0871 200 22 33
Tourist Information Centre 01690 710426 or www.betws-y-coed.co.uk

About the author, David Berry

David is an experienced walker with a love of the countryside and an interest in local history. He is the author of a series of walks guidebooks covering North Wales, where he has lived and worked for many years, and been a freelance writer for Walking Wales magazine. He has also worked as a Rights of Way surveyor across North Wales and served as a member of Denbighshire Local Access Forum. For more information visit:www.davidberrywalks.co.uk

THE COUNTRYSIDE CODE

- Be safe – plan ahead and follow any signs
- Leave gates and property as you find them
- Protect plants and animals, and take your litter home
- Keep dogs under close control
- Consider other people

Open Access
Some routes cross areas of land where walkers have the legal right of access under The CRoW Act 2000 introduced in May 2005. Access can be subject to restrictions and closure for land management or safety reasons for up to 28 days a year. Details from: www.naturalresourceswales.gov.uk. Please respect any notices.

Published by
Kittiwake-Books Limited
3 Glantwymyn Village Workshops,
Glantwymyn, Machynlleth, Montgomeryshire
SY20 8LY
© Text & map research: David Berry 2011
© Maps & illustrations: Kittiwake 2011
Drawings by Morag Perrott
Cover photographs by David Berry. *Main:* Llyn Elsi. *Inset:* Llanrwst Mine Engine House.
Care has been taken to be accurate.
However neither the author nor the publisher can accept responsibility for any errors which may appear, or their consequences. If you are in any doubt about access, check before you proceed.
Printed by Mixam UK..
ISBN: **978 1 902302 96 6**